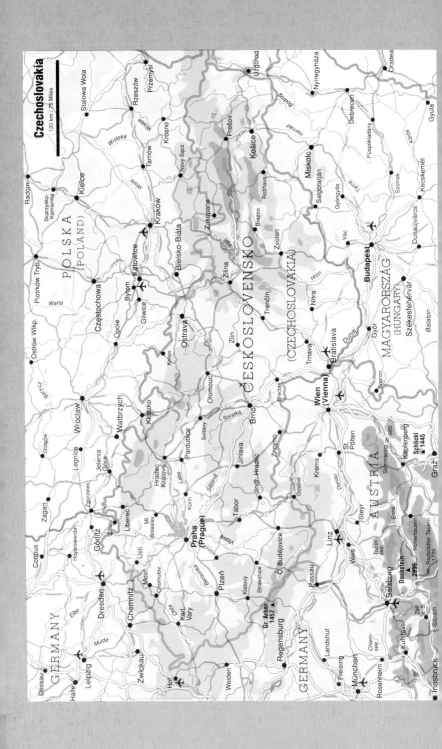

Dobrý den!

This is a guide book that takes you straight to the heart of the ancient city of Prague in the company of three people who know the city intimately, and who want to show you the best it has to offer.

Between them, Alfred Horn, Kerstin Rose and Jan Jelinek know all you'll need to know about Prague, particularly if you only have two or three days to spare: where to go, what to see, what to eat, drink and buy, where to stay and how to get around – all this and more is in these pages.

Your three hosts are led by Alfred Horn, a German journalist who specialises in Eastern Europe and who has already edited a couple of *Insight Guides* on the region. Horn loves Prague and has been travelling to the city since 1965. In these pages he has written the history section, the three day itineraries around the Old City, Hradčany Castle and the New City, and the excursions to Tábor, Pilsen (home of pilsener beer) and the spa town of Carlsbad.

Kerstin Rose, Horn's colleague and co-author, stayed a month in Prague so that she could take a fresh and insightful look behind the scenes of this many-faceted city. For you, the visitor, she took on the task of writing the chapters on culture, the suggestions for short excursions, and hers are the valuable tips in the *Practical Information* section.

Your third host is Prague native Jan Jelinek, who works as a journalist for a daily paper. He and his friends contributed to all its pages, opening doors for the authors and photographers that would otherwise have stayed closed.

Over the last few months prior to publication, this team – effectively your hosts – combed the city of Prague to bring their information absolutely up-to-date. They discovered new restaurants, new nightlife and new hotels – and realised that their favourite city was changing very fast. *Insight Pocket Guide: Prague* is thus the ideal companion for your journey – but use it soon, before everything changes once again in this beautiful, fragile capital.

Dobrý den! Welcome!

Insight Pocket Guide: Prague

First Edition

© **1992 Apa Publications (HK) Ltd**

All Rights Reserved

Printed in Singapore by:
Höfer Press (Pte) Ltd, Singapore

INSIGHT *POCKET* GUIDES

PRAGUE

Authors **Alfred Horn** *and* **Kerstin Rose**
Photographer **Hansjörg Künzel**

INSIGHT
POCKET
GUIDES

Contents

Alfred Horn

Dear Reader

When we prepared for our class trip to Prague in 1965, the city still lay in another world; the Iron Curtain was firmly drawn. In those days, television briefly penetrated the barrier: the fascinating shows of the *Laterna Magika*; exciting films from the Barrandov studios; Emil Zatopek, the racing wonder, and the Dukla Prague ice hockey team. And that was all: the media revealed virtually nothing else.

Before that first school trip, our teacher made us aware for the first time that both Franz Kafka and Heinrich Mann had lived in the city we were going to, and that Schiller's Wallenstein had actually dwelt in a palace on Hradčany. Our teacher also reminded us that Emperor Charles IV had ruled the giant Holy Roman Empire from his native city of Prague, and that relationships between Czechoslovakia and our own native Germany had been far from good. We became a bit nervous.

Then the big day arrived: the train journey to Prague, and the customs officer's scrutiny of the things we were bringing in: nylon shirts, Elvis and Beatles records to give or trade, our own music cassettes, and even a car battery to ensure that our tape recorders would always be ready for use, even in the event of the power failures we'd heard were so common.

When the man at the border ignored our childish contraband, only wondering – in German – that one of our group actually wanted to bring a couple of bottles of beer to Prague, of all places, it was clear that all that awaited us in Prague was a good time.

And that's just how it turned out. We were especially taken with the wonderful pubs and jazz bars; but Smetana's *Moldau*, too, sounded very different to us after we'd walked across the romantic Charles Bridge by moonlight.

In the 25 years since that school outing, I've collected new, continually surprising and varied impressions and memories on every Prague trip. Many things have changed, for Prague, however medieval it may appear, is very much a living metropolis. The 1989 'Velvet Revolution' was an auspicious beginning, but brought harsh upheavals in its wake. The once-tacit understanding between taxi driver and passenger about black market rates has given way to the hard-nosed economic market logic of supply and demand. Prices have risen so dramatically that, although they're still relatively affordable for the traveller, they're beyond the means of many Prague residents. Nonetheless, most of the citizens have managed to maintain their sense of humour.

Despite, or because of, everything, Prague is my city: the most beautiful, most romantic, most fascinating one I know. Anyone who's been there, even for a day, will understand what I mean.

From Village to Metropolis

Every romantic city has to have a legend about its founding. Prague's has been handed down to us by the chronicler Cosmas. He tells of Libuše, a woman as beautiful as she was clever, who drew her beloved Přemysl into the bonds of matrimony and the annals of history. The wild bachelor became positively sedate, and founded a city on the River Moldau 'in which, one day, two olive trees will grow up to the seventh heaven, and shine throughout the world with portents and wonder'.

Their descendants, the Přemyslids, had emerged dominant over

Painting of the Siege of Prague

other family clans as early as the 9th century, and ruled great sections of Bohemia and Moravia from their castle 'Praha' on the left bank of the Moldau. A hundred years later, the erection of Vyšehrad in the south and Hradčany on the heights opposite established the borders of today's city. Bohemia was part of the German Empire and Prague, accordingly, had access to Western Europe and became an important hub for international trade. Bohemia supported Emperor Henry IV in his claim to the throne; as a gesture of gratitude, the monarch rewarded Duke Vratislav II for his allegiance by making him King of Bohemia in 1085.

King of Bohemia

The Přemyslid Princes of Prague proceeded to renovate and strengthen their fortress, expanded St. Vitus' Basilica, founded the Premonstratensian monastery on the Strahov and the Johannite monastery in the Lesser City, and, at the foot of the castle hill, established an additional city for those Germans who had come into the country. On the opposite river bank, in the area of today's Old City Square, Czech merchants and craftsmen embarked on a feverish burst of building activity. A separate city grew up, today known as the Old City or 'Staré Město', complete with a protective wall, craftsmen's guilds, and, after 1338, a new town hall. The free citizens governed their own community; only the so-called 'Jewish Quarter' was directly controlled by the King.

The rapid development on both banks meant that a stone bridge was soon desperately needed. One was begun in 1170, in roughly the position of today's Charles Bridge. By 1300, this first 'Judith Bridge' connected, in addition to two castle complexes, two individual cities. Although they were legally independent of one another and of quite different social characters, with considerable rivalry, both remained flourishing centres of trade.

The death of the last Přemyslid in 1305, and the subsequent struggles for power between foreign candidates for the throne, Bohemian aristocrats and Prague patricians sparked a wave of destruction and plundering. In 1310, nobles and clergymen elected the Emperor's son Johann of Luxemburg their King.

Johann further bolstered his claim to the throne by marrying

Elizabeth, the sister of the last Přemyslid. He had, however, no interest in Prague; and when trade routes were re-routed along the Danube by way of Vienna, the city was cut off from foreign trade and began to decline into a mere provincial backwater.

Emperor Charles IV

But winds of change began to blow with the entrance onto the scene of the son of the Luxemburg duke, who was later to become Charles IV.

Born in Prague, Charles was raised in the court of the French King. When, at the age of 17, he returned to Prague as his father's regent, he industriously set about expanding the city of his childhood. His election as German King in 1349, and his coronation as Emperor in Rome in 1355, conferred upon Prague the status of Imperial Residence. The city blossomed into a metropolis, and became a political and cultural centre.

Several architectural features were established. Construction of the massive, three-nave St Vitus' Cathedral was begun on the foundations of the old basilica. Another of the city's trademarks, the 516m (1,692ft) Charles Bridge, was built in 1357 under the supervision of Peter Parler, Imperial Court Builder. Most significant among the building projects of this period, however, was the establishment of the New City, 'Nové Město', which was laid out in a semicircle around the Old City.

On 8 March 1348, Charles signed the charter which founded the new Prague, and immediately had a protective wall built around the expanded, 800-ha (2000-acre) larger city. Tax incentives induced many new residents to build houses within 18 months, helping the city to develop quickly from a plan on a drawing-board to a bustling centre of business.

But Charles didn't only want to build: he also hoped to make his city into a cultural centre. One of the few highly-educated rulers of the Middle Ages, he knew how to attract the leading minds of the time to his side as aides, advisers, builders and teachers. A mere month after the founding of the New City, on 7 April 1348, he signed the charter for the first university in Central Europe. Professors and students came to the city from all over the world.

Charles' death in 1378 marked the end of an era, and with it came the outbreak of previously dormant conflicts between social and national groups, plunging a city which had become the cultural and political centre of Europe into decline.

The Hussites

The Czech reformer Jan Hus, who became a professor of philosophy at the University of Prague in 1398, spoke out with considerable vigour against the secularisation of the church. He drew much support from the common folk, from citizens of Prague, and even from the King himself, so that what had apparently started merely as a theological dispute rapidly developed into a widespread social and national movement.

In 1409, Hus was able to convince the King to alter the University's charter in such a way that Czech academics would be assured of a majority. Accordingly, all the German scholars withdrew from Prague. The clergy and patricians, shocked at these revolutionary social ideas, reacted by imprisoning and suppressing the Hussites. Jan Hus himself was brought before the Council of Constance, where he was – in spite of assurances of safe conduct – burned at the stake in 1415.

This occasioned a storm of protest in Prague and Bohemia. On 30 July, 1419, an angry mob stormed the Town Hall, demanding the release of a group of imprisoned Hussites. When their demands were not met, the crowd threw a number of officials from the windows, establishing the tradition of 'Prague defenestrations'.

Having routed the clergy and patricians, the Hussites proceeded to elect their own officials and take over the administration of the city. Hussite troops liberated Bohemia, repeatedly conquering Imperial armies. But the movement split, and the 'Utraquists', supported by the Czech nobility and the wealthy middle classes, made peace with the Catholics and the Empire. In 1458, George of Poděbrady, a Czech Utraquist, was crowned King of Bohemia. Destroyed and reduced to an economic shambles during the revolution, the city of Prague experienced a second flowering.

Jan Hus on his way to the pyre in Constance

The Habsburgs

However, dreams of freedom and political autonomy were only realised for a brief two generations. In a portentous Royal Election, the quarrelling Bohemian factions decided, against all historical logic, to choose the Archduke Ferdinand I. This Catholic Habsburg wanted, of all things, to prepare the Bohemian Hussites and their capital city for war with the Protestant German princes. When the citizenry of Prague refused to go along with this, Ferdinand sent in soldiers to plunder the city on 8 July 1547, removed all the privileges won by the Hussite Revolution, and restored the Catholic Church to its former position of power.

Unexpectedly, a new era dawned for the city when Rudolf II (1576–1611) moved the Habsburg residence to Prague, whither he was followed by a swarm of diplomats, merchants, scientists and artists. Engrossed by his hobby of collecting art, Rudolf paid little attention to the city's affairs, and finally had to concede the Bohemian crown to his brother. Prague's citizens tried to gain from the family dispute, and in fact managed to win some concessions, but the fundamental conflict between foreign Catholic rulers and nationalistic, Hussite vassals was far from resolved.

Count Albrecht von Wallenstein

The fuse of revolution was lit, and when, on 23 May 1618, three more city officials were thrown out of the castle windows – 'according to an old Czech tradition', as a voice cried from the angry crowd – the powder-keg exploded. The Thirty Years' War began, and Bohemia and its still-blooming metropolis drew the short straw. For a brief time, the Habsburgs were driven out, and their arch-enemy, Frederick the Elector of the Palatinate, was proclaimed King of Bohemia.

But in November 1620 the united armies of the Emperor and the Catholic League marched into the city and Prague's dreams of being a world power were at an end. For three centuries, the Habsburgs governed all of Central Europe from their capital in Vienna; Prague, humbled, had to be satisfied with the role of provincial capital. At least a generously-appointed palace or two were built, such as that of Count Albrecht von Wallenstein, and a couple of magnificent Baroque churches also came into being during this period, signalling the victory of the Counter-Reformation. Sporadic revolts against the Empire were palliated by social reforms, notably the abolition of serfdom in 1781.

Czech Nationalism

With the beginning of the industrial age, Prague flowered anew, attracting many new Czech citizens. In 1848, the year of revolution, these latter went to the barricades together with the German minority.

But the invitation to the first German Parliament in Frankfurt divided the revolutionaries: the Germans wanted to enter the democratic republic, while the Czechs invited other Slavic delegations to an international congress to discuss the formation of an independent nation.

Synagogue and Jewish town hall, 1890

After the victory of the revolution, the Czech nationalist movement became centred in Prague. In 1861, a Czech was elected mayor for the first time; 20 years later, the public celebrated the opening of the National Theatre, built with donations from the entire population, with a gala performance of Smetana's *Libuše*.

Czechoslovakia was proclaimed a republic in 1918; there was jubilation in Prague at the return of the folk heroes Masaryk and Beneš from exile. An agreement was reached with the Slovaks about the formation of a union, making Prague, once again, a lively capital city. Between the two World Wars, Prague was a cosmopolitan, tolerant city. Classics of the film-maker's art issued from Barrandov's studios, while the large number of magazines and books in circulation were enriched by the contributions of German exiles: Heinrich Mann, for example, received Czech citizenship in 1936.

Hitler's invasion of Czechoslovakia in 1938

National Memorial on Wenceslas Square

The Munich Pact of 1938 sealed the fate of the First Republic and led to six years of oppression in the German 'Imperial Protectorate for Bohemia and Moravia'. When the Germans pulled out of Prague at the end of World War II, they set the north wing of the Town Hall in the Old City on fire. The Russian Red Army was welcomed into Prague, and the Communists were able to take power in 1948 virtually without effort. But Stalinist terror, coupled with ignorance and incompetence, soon destroyed all hope of the Czechs finding a path to socialism.

The Prague Spring

The 'Prague Spring' of 1968 took root in long years of wintry frost, in which an increasing number of writers and dramatists spoke out with criticisms it was impossible to ignore. Their words fell on historically fertile ground in Prague, and gave rise to a movement which it took a Russian invasion to quell.

But the spark lit in Prague continued to glow, fanned into flames by the Solidarity movement in Gdansk, Poland, and leading finally to the bonfire of reform in Moscow. Scarcely 10 years later, the human rights group Charta 77 was formed and showed that it was possible to stand tall even within a system which had little respect for human dignity. Co-founder Václav Havel, poet and playwright, was made the leader of 1989's 'Velvet Revolution' almost against his will.

Václav Havel

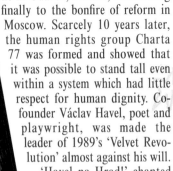

'Havel na Hrad!' chanted the crowds during those November days, and elevated their poet and playright to power.

Historical Highlights

25,000 BC A highly-developed Stone Age culture moves into Southern Moravia and leaves behind the Venus of Věstonice, the oldest ceramic in the world.

ca 1,000 BC Celts settle on the Moldau.

1st century BC German tribes settle and hold their own against the Roman Empire.

6th century AD Slavic tribes drive out the Germans and settle.

623–4 The Frankish merchant and war hero Samo is crowned King, his Slavic army drives out Frankish invaders. Samo's empire dissolves after his death.

9th century The sixth empire is formed. According to legend, Přemysl and Libuše found the new Czech dynasty.

907 Invading Hungarians take over Slovakia, which remains in their possession until 1918.

1029 Václav – Wenceslas I, the Holy – Christianises the country, preparing the way for unification of Bohemia and Moravia.

1212 With the 'Golden Bull of Bohemia', Emperor Friedrich II makes the unified land into a hereditary kingdom.

1306 End of Přemyslid dynasty.

1316 Charles IV born in Prague.

1333 Charles IV's father gives him responsibility for Bohemia and Moravia.

1348 First university in Central Europe opens in Prague.

1355 Pope Innocent VI crowns Charles IV Emperor in Rome. Prague becomes capital.

ca 1400 Charles's son Wenceslas IV is criticised by the Czech pastor Jan Hus, who also attacks the secularisation of the church.

1415 Hus is burned as a heretic.

1419 Revolt against the German upper class. Hussites demand a Czech national state.

1458 George of Poděbrady is the last ruler of Czech nationality.

1526 The Bohemians elect the Habsburg Ferdinand King. The Habsburgs govern Bohemia, Moravia and Slovakia until 1918.

1583 Rudolf II moves his residence from Vienna to Hradčany.

1618 Angry citizens throw imperial administrators from the palace windows, sparking the Thirty Years' War.

1918 Czech Republic, joined with Slovakia, is proclaimed. Tomás G Masaryk elected first President.

1938 Munich Pact. Hitler uses the alleged discrimination against the German minority in Czechoslovakia as an excuse to invade.

1939 Creation of the 'Imperial Protectorate of Bohemia and Moravia'.

1945 Prague is liberated by the Red Army.

1948 In a free election, the Communist Party receives 38 per cent of the vote, and the country becomes the Socialist Republic of Czechoslovakia.

1968 Warsaw Pact tanks crush Alexander Dubček's 'Prague Spring'.

1977 Founding of the civil rights group Charta 77.

1989 The 'Velvet Revolution' brings a free and federalist constitution to Czechoslovakia. Václav Havel, Speaker of the Citizens' Forum, is elected President. But the inherited problems are not yet resolved. The country's rebirth is hampered by painful economic reforms and Slovakia's call for its own independence.

Prague is an international centre for mime

Culture in Bohemia's Capital

Two dozen theatres, three opera houses, 24 museums, and a growing number of galleries – Prague is home to all of these. In this creative city, every day sees the ripening of new ideas, concepts and projects emerging in the arts. Throughout centuries of oppression, literature, music and the visual arts were often the only ways to preserve national identity and to keep alive the hope of independence and freedom.

The composer Bedřich Smetana, renowned in Prague during his lifetime, was one of the most determined of Czech nationalists. His symphonic poems such as the *Moldau, Libuše* and *Má Vlast* (My Fatherland) were his means of giving expression to the national cultural identity. Since 1946, the famous 'Prague Spring' music festival has always begun on 12 May, the day of Smetana's death, and the opening concert takes place in the Smetana Hall of the Municipal House.

Throughout the year, people busily make music in private apartments, palaces and churches. The popularity of music in Prague, both private and public, was noted as early as 1772 by the English musicologist Dr Charles Burney, who claimed that the Czechs were 'the most musical people of Europe'. And, although rock and pop have long been able to establish and maintain their popularity and concerts in Prague's Cultural Palace are regularly sold out, classical music continues to play a major role in the city's cultural life.

Literature has also been an influential force on Prague's cultural scene. Jaroslav Hašek and Franz Kafka, representatives of an entire epoch of literary history, used satire and parable in order to be able to express themselves without interference from the censors. Their successors under communist dictatorship had it no better, particularly after 1968, when there was a continual threat of blacklisting or imprisonment. Contemporary writers like Milan Kundera, Josef Škvorecký and Ludvík Vaculík went into exile or struggled to earn a living as cooks or street-cleaners.

Not until the 'Velvet Revolution' of 1989 was it possible to buy the books of these authors within their own country. And the people's thirst to make up for what they've missed seems unquenchable: first or new editions of works by these once-proscribed countrymen are generally sold out within a few hours. It's no coincidence, then, that a playwright, Václav Havel, was elected President in 1989, and that other people from the Prague cultural scene today occupy high offices.

Even the old guard of Prague artists who were able to avoid being blacklisted are now ready and able to realise old dreams. Boris Hybner is in the process of expanding his newly-founded theatre Gag with an international mime school, and the renowned jazz musician Milan Svoboda wants to help Czech jazz to reach an international audience.

The creative energy of the Czechs and Slovaks is also evident in film. In the 1960s, Miloš Forman and Jiří Menzel attracted international notice. Today, the Barrandov Studios, near Prague, produce imaginative films such as Menzel's *Love to a Timetable*, which displays both lyrical talent and biting humour.

The spectacular *Laterna Magika*, presented at the theatre Nová Scéna, offers a synthesis of film, pantomime and acting. Located next to this theatre, the old National Theatre is a symbol of the independent cultural movement and the Slavia coffeehouse opposite has long been a meeting-place for the city's 'scene'. In Prague, political developments are steered by art and culture, not the other way round. Artists passionately treasure their responsibility to society, and are often spokesmen for other, less privileged, fellow-citizens. Prague residents are equally passionate in their identification with their artists: they discuss them, criticise them, and love them. There's hardly another city in which art and culture play such a role in everyday life as they do in the capital of Czechoslovakia.

Hard Times

The golden dreams of the 'Velvet Revolution' haven't yet faded, but many Prague citizens are finding it hard to adjust to the realities of a capitalist economy.

Inflation is rampant. It seems that only those who have foreign capital will be able to survive. Anyone with a fixed salary – which averages only 5,000 crowns – be he or she an engineer, architect or doctor, legal assistant or street-cleaner, is having a difficult time. Those who were able to 'put aside' foreign currency under the communist regime have emerged as the winners in this time of upheaval. As a result, Prague's social tables are turning in a most unusual manner: former waiters and taxi-drivers, as well as currency traders, are the financial winners of the revolution, not the aristocrats. A new, well-to-do class – the owners of boutiques, restaurants and exchange offices – has sprung up out of thin air. These were the only people who were able, in the course of 'small privatisation', to bid for houses, small businesses and shops which didn't have previous owners to claim them, and thus to put themselves in a position to profit from tourism.

'Large privatisation', which involves transforming city businesses, newspapers, film studios and radio stations into shareholders' corporations, still lies in the future. And whether those who lost out in the course of the 'small privatisation' will have any interest in partaking in the purchase of stocks is questionable, to say the least. The Škoda automobile plant has already been sold to the German firm Volkswagen.

Even those who hope to receive damages for losses suffered will be disappointed. As yet, no binding regulations have been established as to the amount of such damages. One thing only is certain: payment will be made in crowns – and you can't buy anything with those, anyway. And anyone still in possession of their former resources will not have much reason to celebrate. If a house was renovated by the city within the last decade, the government is now demanding repayment for the work undertaken – and who can afford that, with the low salaries paid in the city today?

Under such conditions, few citizens are bothered by the fact that it's hardly possible to breathe the air of Prague, particularly under certain weather conditions. The cost of clearing up the pollution resulting from decades of disregard for the environment is bound to be a drain on an already heavily taxed future.

Many houses need renovation

The city needs entrepreneurial initiative

More immediately noticeable is the fact that the crime rate has risen dramatically since 1989. In the 'open city', purse-snatching and prostitution, often prompted by acute need, are no longer rarities and visitors should take care.

For many Eastern Europeans seeking work, Prague is a station on the route into the 'golden' West. Most of this migrant population are without means, and have no way to support themselves other than to resort to illegal methods. Their small-scale crimes of palming off counterfeit money or Yugoslavian dinars on tourists who are exchanging money on the black market is still relatively harmless compared to some of the alternatives.

The problem of prostitution has been augmented by the presence of Western tourists. More than 25,000 practitioners of the world's oldest profession – often the only way to obtain Western money – are said to operate along the Moldau, particularly in discos and the bars of major hotels. Furthermore, a number of establishments appropriate to the trade have sprung up around Wenceslas Square.

With such economic circumstances, who could blame the locals for preferring to stay at home in the evening rather than venture out for their entertainment? The city's traditional cultural organisations, the many small theatres and concert halls, have suffered badly as a result.

Often, because of local economics, spoken drama yields its place to pantomime, *Laterna Magika*-style theatre or to jazz concerts – events which are tailored to the demands of Western tourists, with their more ample financial resources.

Times are none too rosy for most of the people of Prague. Yet they refuse to give up, and deal equably with the social turbulence around them. They haven't relinquished their sly humour, nor their hopes for better times ahead. After all, Prague has been written off in the past – only to rise again in even greater splendour.

Orientation

It's not difficult to find your way around in Prague; the most important sights, at least, can be reached on foot. The centre of the city ('Praha 1') is divided into the historic quarters of Lesser City (Malá Strana), Old City (Staré Město), and New City (Nové Město). The Lesser City is on the left bank of the Moldau (Vltava), and is augmented by another self-enclosed quarter, the fortress of Hradčany.

Linked to Hradčany by the celebrated old Charles Bridge (Karlův most), the untrafficked streets of the Old City are surrounded by the busy Old City Ring (Staroměstské náměstí). Once markedly different in appearance, the Jewish quarter, known as Josefov or Židovské Město, is today completely integrated into the Old City.

The New City, Nové Město, is laid out in a semicircle around the Old City, and the central axis of this busy neighbourhood is the famous Wenceslas Square. A futuristic underground line links the city centre with the suburbs, and provides well-thought-out transportation within the city itself. Public conveyances include old-fashioned streetcars, especially in the Nové Město. A ride on line 22 will give you an idea of the city's layout.

Most of the best stores are located around Wenceslas Square and in the adjacent street Na příkopě. Restaurants, inns and galleries have settled primarily in the Staré Město.

The Old City

A stroll through the winding streets of the Old City. After enjoying the tranquillity of the Jewish cemetery and the bustle of the Old City Square, dine in style in Paříž.

On the first day I suggest you follow the inclination of Prague residents, who prefer, if possible, to begin the day over a long break-

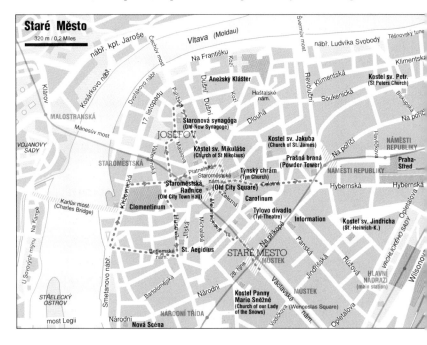

The Town Hall's astronomical clock

fast with the morning paper, or simply chatting with friends.

Wherever you stay in Prague, the starting point of this first day, **Wenceslas Square** (Václavské náměstí), is easy to find. This square – actually more of a broad boulevard – lies on the boundary between the Old City and the New. To the left and right, broad pedestrian zones follow the course of the fortifications which surrounded the city in the Middle Ages, before Charles IV erected the New City in a semicircle around the old.

Take the small street **Na můstku** which leads directly into the colourful life of the Old City. Only a few paces along, you'll stumble on a **flea market**, where stalls offer all manner of second-hand wares, pirate cassette tapes, books, and hot dogs. The Melantrichova leads directly to the **Old City Town Hall** (Staroměstská radnice) with its famous clock tower, dating from 1410. Here, a brief look at the **Old City Square** with its churches, palaces and splendid residential houses; you'll come back here in the afternoon.

Particularly notable is the Town Hall's **astronomical clock**, which preserves the medieval view of the course of the sun and moon upon its face: the earth is at the centre of the universe. At the very top of the clock, Death appears every hour to strike the bells and let the hourglass of life run out; the Apostles march past him, while a rooster crows.

Beyond the Town Hall – which today only has a decorative function – you'll come to a fountain with a lovely Renaissance grille and a typical Old Prague hardware store. Following the bend in the Karlova ul, you'll see the **Clam-Gallas Palace** (Clam-Gallasův palác) on the **Husova** to your right; the building is a well-restored High Baroque residential home, which now houses the city archives. Going south along the Husova, you'll come to the **Bethlehem Chapel** (Betlémská kaple) by taking the third street on the right; Jan Hus used to deliver his fiery sermons against bigotry and ostentation in this simple house of worship.

Next door, you can visit the pastor's house, where a permanent exhibition documents the life and work of the great reformer. On

Smetana

the west side of the square (Betlémské nám.), the building housing the **Ethnological Museum** (Náprstkovo muzeum) surrounds a picturesque courtyard.

The Náprstkova leads to the Moldau. Here, beyond the embankment, a small terrace in front of the **Smetana Museum** (Muzeum Bedřicha Smetany) offers perhaps the most well-known vantage point for photographers of **Charles Bridge** (Karlův most) and **Hradčany**.

Passing the former mill-houses, we come to the **Old City Bridge Tower** and the **Church of St Francis**, also known as the Crusaders' Church, with its magnificently painted dome. Opposite is the baroque facade of **St Salvator**, a part of the sprawling complex of the **Clementinum**. This college of Jesuits, who were summoned into the country in 1556, was the bulkhead of the Counter-Reformation in Hussite Prague. Today, it serves as the city library.

Behind this massive building, the Platnéřská branches off and leads almost back to the Ring. Shortly before you get there, turn off into Zatecká, and you'll find yourself in the **Jewish Quarter**, directly at the entrance of the strangely moving **Jewish Cemetery** with its weathered gravestones and gnarled trees. At the grave of Rabbi Loew, practising Jews honour the great teacher known to us principally as the creator of *The Golem*, the clay monster brought to life by alchemy who went on to spread fear in the ghettoes.

A path running along the cemetery wall leads into a dead-end street. To the left, the old entrance to the cemetery is near the

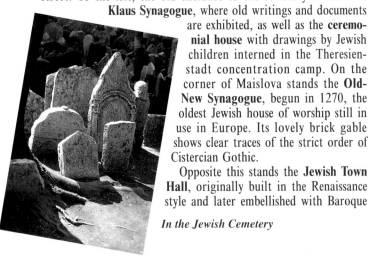

Klaus Synagogue, where old writings and documents are exhibited, as well as the **ceremonial house** with drawings by Jewish children interned in the Theresienstadt concentration camp. On the corner of Maislova stands the **Old-New Synagogue**, begun in 1270, the oldest Jewish house of worship still in use in Europe. Its lovely brick gable shows clear traces of the strict order of Cistercian Gothic.

Opposite this stands the **Jewish Town Hall**, originally built in the Renaissance style and later embellished with Baroque

In the Jewish Cemetery

elements. Have a close look at the gable, with its singular clock with Hebrew numbers: the hands turn counter-clockwise! An entrance off the Maislova leads into the lower town hall, where a **Kosher Restaurant** (Tel: 231 89 96) is open for lunch. Accompanying the simple, hearty fare, the melancholy music of the house pianist could be expressing the mood of the entire quarter. A more genteel and perhaps more cheerful alternative might be the wine cellar-cum-restaurant U **Golema**, Maislova 8 (Tel: 232 81 65), or the pleasant U **Barona** in Pařížská 19 (Tel: 232 72 60).

Before your afternoon begins, have a last look around and note the wonderful art nouveau facades that line Pařížská ; then wander back down this stylish avenue to the Old City Square again. Once there, you will see the ornate facade of **St Nicholas' Church**, built in 1735 by Kilian Ignaz Dientzenhofer, to your right. The Old City Square (Staroměstské náměstí) is the natural mid-point of the Old City, and the heart of Prague. The **Jan Hus Monument**, erected on 6 July 1915, on the 500th anniversary of his death, somewhat detracts from the effect of its striking breadth, but **Týn Church** still towers over all, forming a breathtaking backdrop.

On the north side of the square you'll find historic **House No 7**, once a monastery of the Pauline monks; on the east side, the **Kinsky Palace** presents a facade decidedly influenced by the Rococo. At the foot of the church towers are, adjacent to one another, the Gothic **House at the Stone Bell**, **Týn School**, and the **House at the**

Old City Square

White Unicorn. Týn School, with its facilities for rotating exhibitions, and Celetná ul 5 provide the two entrances to **Týn Church**, most noteworthy for its Bohemian Baroque paintings and the oldest baptismal font in Prague. Behind the church, an alley leads left from the Štupartská to the **Church of St James**. Built by the Minorites during the reign of Charles IV, this building was renovated during the Baroque period. With a little luck, you may ave an op-

The Powder Tower

portunity to tune yourself in to this beautiful building by catching one of the many recitals given on the wonderfully decorated, uniquely-toned organ built in 1705 (check the poster by the door for times).

Returning to Celetná, stroll a part of the way along this former 'Royal Way'. At the beginning of the street is the **Egon Erwin Kisch Café**. In the 1920s, this Prague journalist came to fame as the 'roving reporter'; it is less well-known that he was one of the few German-language writers to continue to work in the city after the war. As an author, too, he set particularly high standards. Perhaps you can see some of his works in the two bookshops which you will come across on the left side of the street.

At the end of the Celetná towers the mighty **Powder Tower** (Prašná brána). On the very spot where a fortified tower protected the old city in the 13th century, King Jagiello had a new defensive construction erected directly beside his royal residence in 1475 but its importance diminished after the royal residence was moved to Hradčany. The Tower's name derives from its use as a powder magazine in the 18th century. The building was renovated at the end of the last century, when a new roof was added; from the top, which is reached by a long spiral case, the visitor can enjoy a lovely view over the Old City, which fills up with pedestrians in the early evening hours.

Just next door, on the site of the former Royal Court, the art nouveau building of the **Municipal House** shelters a café, a restaurant, a wine-cellar and a concert hall all gathered together under one roof. For the moment, put off a visit to this complex until another day and, instead, conclude your day's tour with a stylish dinner in the well-known restaurant **Paříž** (Tel: 232 20 51), which is located behind the Municipal House in a building dating from 1907; as well as the original decor, this venue provides a first encounter with the cuisine of Bohemia – here refined with a touch of French sophistication.

Charles Bridge, Lesser City and Hradčany Castle

From the Old City Bridge Tower across the river over Charles Bridge to Lesser City Square for lunch. Up the elegant Nerudova to Hradčany Castle and St Vitus's Cathedral. In the evening: typical Lesser City food and drink.

This day's sightseeing begins at about 9am atop the **Old City Bridge Tower** (Staroměstská mostecká věž). In the morning mists, the city on either side of the Moldau (Vltava) has the appearance of a stage set, blurred by a fog of make-believe.

Behind you lies the Old City, the centre of bourgeois Prague, where knowledge and trade flowered and gave rise to an international, cosmopolitan culture.

On the other side of the river, the city has another face. The **Lesser City** (Malá Strana), immediately on the opposite bank, used to be a neighbourhood of simple workers, carters and fishermen, yet it was built in the shadow of the rulers' residential city. The elaborate palaces of aristocrats, monasteries, churches, and the imperial Cathedral were all crowded atop the cliffs of **Hradčany**. The whole was dominated by the Castle, home of the ruling families for a good thousand years.

By building **Charles Bridge** (Karlův most), Charles IV hoped to

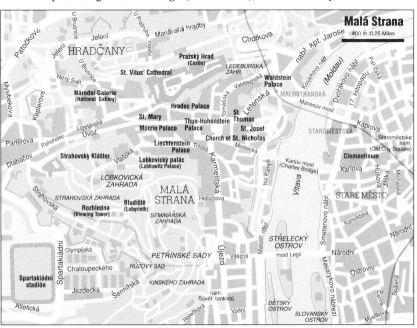

Charles Bridge

link the two rival settlements, on opposite riverbanks, into a single city. The magnificent stone bridge built by Peter Parler is the central section of the 'Royal Way' (see *Pick & Mix* Itinerary 1). Upstream, sculpted Baroque saints gaze upon the untiring play of the waters below them. The scene seems to demand the music of Smetana's *Moldau*.

On the right, meanwhile, the silhouette of the Castle, crowned by the shape of St Vitus' Cathedral, is sharply etched against the sky.

On the other end of the bridge, the **Lesser City Bridge Tower** (Malostranská mostecká věž) awaits visitors. To the right, beneath the bridge, is a romantic inn called the **Three Ostriches Hotel** (U tří pštrosů), Drazického nám. 12 (Tel: 53 61 51). Here, good money will get you a room – Goethe laid his head upon these pillows – and, if you reserve in time, a good meal as well.

Just past the city gate you turn left into **Lázeňská**, passing the former luxury hotels **Spa** (v Lázních) and the **Golden Unicorn** (U zlatého jednorožce), and soon coming to the oldest Lesser City church, **St Mary-under-the-Chain** (Kostel Panny Marie pod řetězem) with its ponderous Romanesque-Gothic facade.

On the neighbouring square, Velokopřevorské náměstí, the **Maltese Grand Prior's Palace** houses an enchanting collection of musical instruments. The Palace's gardens border on the Moldau island of **Kampa** (Na Kampě), which can be reached by means of a small bridge over the **Devil's Stream** (Čertovka). In the last decades, this 'little Venice' with its romantic water-mills and gardens was the meeting-place of Prague's children of the sixties, whose wall paintings can still be admired today (see below).

Next you go back through Maltese Square (Maltézské nám.) with its stately **Nostitz Palace** (Nostický palác), which today serves as the Ministry of Culture. Right on Karmelitská, the **Vrtba Palace** (Vrtbovský palác), No 25, is worth a look, above all for its terraced gardens. On Mostecká, Bridge Street, you turn left onto the **Lesser City Square** (Malostranské nám), where the mighty **Church of St Nicholas** (Kostel sv Mikuláše) raises its twin towers. Every detail of its interior, from the majestic ceiling murals to the pulpit and the ornately embellished chancel, reflects the demand for absolutism which characterised the victorious Catholic Church in the Counter-Reformation – a sharp contrast to the simple Bethlehem Chapel of preacher and heretic Jan Hus.

After so much opulence, you are sure to be hungry. Around the square there are several places where you can discover the charms of hidden corners, courtyards, and passageways. The élite wine restaurant **U Mecenáše** (No 10) doesn't open until 5pm, and is really more appropriate for evening dining (reservations recommended), but the Renaissance building in which it's housed is

Facades on the Mostecká, Bridge Street

worth a look. At this time of day, there's more chance of finding a seat in **U Glaubičů** (No 5). New eateries are constantly opening in the area's picturesque back courtyards: try exploring them yourself. If you don't find anything, there's always the **Café** on the square, where, if the weather's fine, you can sit outdoors and marvel at the way the trams take the curves at speed; there's also a fine view of the **Town Hall** (No 21) and the **Montag House** (No 18), also known as the Smiřický Palace, where the second and most significant 'Prague defenestration' was planned in 1618.

Fortified by lunch, you should now ascend the steep street Nerudova ul toward the Castle. Once the main road up to the Castle, Nerudova is lined with dozens of mansions from every architectural epoch. The imaginatively-decorated facades help mark the route: a golden cup hangs from the **House of the Golden Goblet** (U zlaté číše, No 16), and three violins from the **House of the Three Vio-**

lins (U tří housliček, No 34). Particularly remarkable in the lower section of Nerudova are the impressive portal and the balcony supported by statues of Moors which adorn the **Morzin Palace** (Morzinsky palác, No 5).

At the upper end, Nerudova narrows into a romantic stairway, which leads up to **Hradčanské nám**. The magnificent buildings on this square once formed an independent community which was under the control of the Castle rulers. To the left of the stairs, the Renaissance edifice of the former **Town Hall** is adorned with the Imperial and state coats of arms. Here, Loretánská leads off to the left toward the Loreto church and the formerly poor neighbourhood of Nový Svět (New World); we've planned a tour of these areas for another day (see *Pick & Mix* Itinerary 3). You shouldn't, however, pass up a visit to the **Schwarzenberg Palace**, less for the military museum therein than for its wonderful ceiling murals on the second floor. You can only see the distinctive **Archbishop's Palace** (Arcibiskupský palác) if you happen to arrive there on the Thursday before Easter. The Bishop's family settled down comfortably in a splendid palace behind his own.

Over a thousand years old, **Hradčany Castle** (Pražský Hrad) was a residence of the early Přemyslid rulers, who established their headquarters in this strategic position over the Moldau. Genera-

The Archbishop's Palace

tions of rulers continued to expand the complex with churches and palaces, defensive and residential buildings.

You enter the castle through the first, historically most recent, courtyard, and stand before the Baroque **St Matthew's Gateway** (Matyášova brána). To the right, a staircase leads up to the throne room, where the President of the Republic now receives diplomatic guests. More interesting is the second courtyard, with the lovely

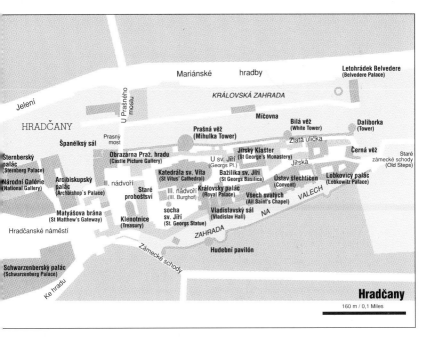

fountain and the **Chapel of the Holy Rood**, which contains the church treasury. Here, too, you'll find the **Rudolf Gallery.** The last Prague Emperor, Rudolf II, was a passionate collector. Ignoring the disparaging smiles of his contemporaries, he assembled marvellous objects, exotic stuffed animals, alchemists' tools, and shamanistic cult figures. Although the collection was strewn to the four winds by war and theft and most of the remaining items were moved to Vienna, the gallery is still worth a visit.

A portal in the north wing will lead you to the beautifully laid-out **Royal Gardens** (Královská zahrada), which, although renamed the Presidential Garden to accord with the democratic spirit, are only open to the public on weekends. If you've come this far, walk on to the Renaissance edifice of the **Royal Summer Palace** (Královsky letohrádek).

From the north side of the Castle's third courtyard, the impressive facade of **St Vitus' Cathedral** (Katedrála sv Víta) will confront the visitor. The interior of the Gothic basilica, at 124m (407ft) long and 60m (197ft) wide the largest church in Prague, is quite simply breathtaking. Begun by Charles IV's architect Matthias von Arras in 1344 and continued by Peter Parler and his sons, the Cathedral has lost none of its splendour over the years, even if the modern stained-glass windows which replace

Entrance to the Castle

the lost originals illuminate the interior with a rather pale light, lacking the mystery one associates with old cathedrals.

In the course of the centuries the building has been added to and modified; construction work stopped, at least for the present, in 1929. From its inception, the cathedral was not only a place of worship, but also a coronation church, mausoleum, witness to historical events, and the goal of nationalist pilgrimages from every corner of the country. Elaborate **St Wenceslas' Chapel**, in the southern transept, is also steeped in national history: everything in it has to do with the life and work of this sainted Bohemian king. A stairway leads to the **Chapel of the Holy Rood**, and down to the remains of an early medieval church and the royal crypt with the sarcophagus of Charles IV.

Broad and majestic, **Vladislav Hall** in the **Old Royal Palace** opposite is customarily entered by way of the Riders' Staircase, used in bygone days by mounted knights entering the hall to take part in tournaments. One annex houses the **Bohemian Chancellery**, from whose windows enraged Bohemians threw the Imperial governors in 1618. Behind the dome rises the mighty **Mihulka Tower**, the Late Gothic fortification of the castle in which you can visit, among other things, an alchemist's laboratory.

After all that you are probably ready for a break. In the castle wall behind the apse you can get a snack in one of the many small eateries. Alternatively, wander along the Golden Lane (Zlatá ulicka) behind **St George's Basilica** (Basilika sv Jiří), where, in addition to a small pub, you'll find antique shops and booksellers in the tiny houses that nestle into the castle wall. Craftsmen, goldsmiths and tailors have lived here for 400 years, their services

The Kafka House on Golden Lane

available for the lords who lived next door. Here, too, you can see the **Kafka House** (No 22).

If you continue down in the direction of the East Gate, you will come to the observation terrace in the shadow of the **Black Tower**. From here, you can descend the Old Castle Steps down to Valdštejnská. Turning left, proceed to the Ledebour Palace (Ledeburský palác), with its small square: here, **Valdšte-jnska Hospode** (Tomásská ul. 16, Tel: 53 61 95) is my tip for authentic Bohemian dining. If you haven't reserved, or can't find a table, go further along Tomásská to the Lesser City Square; on the corner, **U Schnellů** offers evening fare. One hundred metres away, the traditional pub **U Svatého Tomáše** (Letenská 12, Tel: 53 00 64) offers even more authentic cuisine. After that I hope that you have an exhilarating, romantic stroll through the night streets back to your hotel.

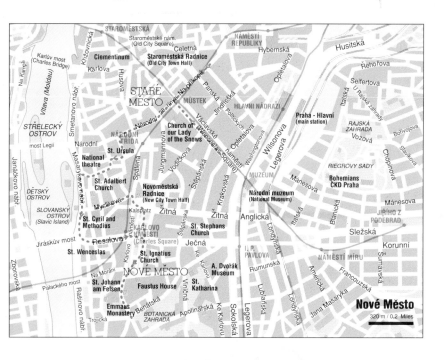

Wenceslas Square and the New City

From Wenceslas Square through the attractions of the New City: shopping precincts, fortifications, the National Theatre and Prague's most famous coffee house. Along the Moldau river for lunch, historic churches and Charles Square. Finishing the day off with a hearty Bohemian meal in U Fleků, or refined Russian fare in Volha.

Today you finally get to see **Wenceslas Square** (Václavské náměstí) probably Prague's most famous place. It's never quiet here even in the early hours of the morning, the paths of the last visitors to the casinos, clubs and discos cross those of early morning commuters.

More of an avenue than a static open square, Wenceslas Square was originally planned as a horse market. It was to form the central business hub of the New City which Charles IV was having built around the Old City which had grown too small. Every revolution in Prague, from the Hussites to the 'Velvet Revolutionaries' in November of 1989, has taken place here. The square has long been the stage for national mobilisations, bitter defeats and uproarious victory celebrations.

The National Museum on Wenceslas Square

Wenceslas Square is dominated by the 100m (328ft) facade of the **National Museum** (Národní muzeum), built between 1885 and 1890 by native Bohemian workmen. As well as a collection of natural history, the building houses a large library. The mighty equestrian **Statue of St Wenceslas** dates from 1913, a reminder of the glory days of the independent Bohemian state.

Start your walk down the left-hand side of the 680-m (2,230-ft) long square. Across the way, the classical art nouveau hotels Evropa, Zlatá Husa and Ambassador provide great snapshot material. On your side of the square, the **Alfa Palace** (No 28), a modernistic building from 1928, and the **Peterka House** (No 12) are both worthy of notice.

At the end of the square, cross over to the **Crown Palace** (Palác Koruna), which combines Constructivist and art nouveau elements. Heading back up the other side of the square, turn left halfway along into Jindřišská in search of refreshment. On the next corner, the **Hotel Palace** has a stylish lobby and elegant first-floor restaurant. Even more interesting is the adjacent **Self-Service Bistro,** where remarkably little money will buy you wonderful small meals, including vegetarian dishes – a rarity in a city whose cuisine is centred on roast pork, cabbage and dumplings!

To the left, **Panská** leads down to Na příkopě, past the main headquarters of the tourist agency Čedok and the private housing agency Hello. If you're looking for cheap accommodation, you've come to the right place: citizens with rooms to let are standing at the doorway, only too happy to offer you a bargain.

The lively pedestrian precinct of **Na příkopě** ia a great place for walking, people-watching and window-shopping. To the right, towards the Powder Tower, you can book plane and rail tickets in the **Čedok** office (No 18) in the morning, get information from the **Prague Information Office** (No 20), or have a bite to eat in the restaurant or bistro of the **Cultural Centre** (No 22). To the left, on the opposite side, you can seek out the two well-stocked bookshops and the childrens' department store **Dětský Dům** (No 15), an interesting building from the late 1920s.

Returning to Wenceslas Square, cross over and bear to the left to get to **Jungmannovo nám.**, a square named after Josef Jungmann (1773–1847), the reviver of the Czech language. Here, you'll see the **Church of Our Lady of the Snows** (Kostel Panny Marie Sněžné), built in 1347. This church became famous as the headquarters of the radical Hussites, who, led by Jan Hus, marched from here to the New City Town Hall in 1419, to teach the conceited governors 'how to behave'.

Bearing again to the right, join the continuation of Na příkopě, **Národní třída**, another lively pedestrian zone. Here stands the modernistic department store **Máj** and the Baroque **Church of St Ursula** (No 8). In the former **Ursuline Convent** (Klášter voršilek), you can combine art appreciation with good eating in the **Convent Wine Cellar** (Klásterní vinárna; Tel: 29 05 96, open 11am–midnight).

The **National Theatre** (Národní divadlo), testimony to the national enthusiasm for culture in the late 19th century, dominates the end of the street. When the auditorium burned down before the theatre was officially opened, Prague's citizens contributed the means necessary to rebuild it within a matter of weeks. Many artists worked without pay on the magnificent decorations.

Opened in 1983, the **Nová Scéna** presents mainly ballet performances, but also stages productions of the *Laterna Magika*. Opposite, the **Café Slavia** commands a wonderful view of the theatre and the Moldau. Time seems to have stood still in this *ne plus ultra* of Prague coffeehouses. Tourists and locals, charming women and clever gigolos keep their trysts over a cup of cappuccino or *café Russe*, entertained by a real orchestra.

Heading upstream along the Moldau (Vltava), you pass the **Slavic Island** (Slovanský ostrov), which has a lovely garden restaurant and a range of evening cultural events, on your right. Stop at the **Mánes House** of visual arts. From the outside, the architecture of this building shows the influence of the Bauhaus; inside, artists' organisations present interesting exhibitions. The beautiful café on the Moldau encourages visitors to stay awhile. If you like things more hearty, or more fishy, go about 200m further on past the old water tower and across the **Jirásek Bridge** (Jiráskův most), and climb the stairs up to the embarkation pier of the Moldau excursion boats. Tucked away up here is the less well-known terrace restaurant **Vltava** (Tel: 29 49 64). On cool days, the **Fisherman's Inn** is a cosy alternative.

Back along the other side of the river, after eating, follow **Resslova** and turn into the second street on the right to come to Romanesque **St Wenceslas' Church** (Kostel sv Václava na Zderaze). The name 'At Zderaz' betrays its origins as the village church of what was once a small community, incorporated into the New City of Prague. Today, the building is home to the nearly inconsequential Czech Hussite church. Diagonally opposite, the crypt of the church of **SS Cyril and Methodius** (Kostel sv Cyrila a Metoděje) was the scene of a bloody battle in May 1942; it was here that the assassins of Reinhard 'the hangman' Heydrich took refuge, fighting to the last man against Nazi pursuers. Today, a memorial to them is housed in this Czech Orthodox church.

You now reach **Charles Square** (Karlovo nám), which was created during the building of the New City and was once the site of the cattle market. On the right, you come to the **Faustus House**, south of the well-tended gardens. Legend has it that this was once the residence of Dr Faustus; but it's a matter of historical fact that it served as home to the English adventurer Edward

In the beer-garden of U Fleků

Kelly, who promised Emperor Rudolf II a lump of gold from his alchemical laboratory.

On Vyšehradská, south of the square, you will stumble across the **Emmaus Monastery** (Klášter na Slovanech). The monastery has played an important role in the city since it was founded by Charles IV, as it controls access to the Moldau. Bombing in World War II destroyed many irreplaceable medieval art treasures here, but the magnificent cloisters alone make the monastery worth a visit.

Back to Charles Square, the centre of which is dominated by **St Ignatius Church** (Kostel sv Ignáce), which has been the Jesuits' main church since 1677. On the square's north side, the stately **New City Town Hall** (Novoměstská radnice) provides a visual balance to the Faustus House opposite.

Watery reflection of Týn church

In 1419, the Hussite Revolution began here, and the infamous tradition of 'Prague defenestrations' was launched. Until 1784, when the four cities of Prague were joined into a single administrative entity, the Town Hall remained the centre of political events in the New City. But now your steps should turn toward **U Fleků** (Křemencova 11, Tel: 29 24 36). Going left from the Town Hall into Myslíkova, then taking the second right into Křemencova, should bring you to the famous clock, the trademark of this renowned Old Prague eatery which every Prague traveller has to have visited at least once. In the summer, a band plays in the outdoor beer garden, but you can also drink in the dim interior, with seating for almost a thousand people: either way, you're sure to get roast pork with dumplings!

If your preference is for something other than the smell of beer, then proceed, instead, to the **Volha** restaurant in Myslíkova 14 (Tel: 29 64 06, 11am–midnight). The quality artwork on the walls match the quality of the attentive service and the excellent menu. Bon appetit!

1. The Royal Way

A walk through the Old City and Lesser City.

'The Royal Way' became the common designation for this thoroughfare in the 14th century, when it was the shortest route between the Royal Court built by King Wenceslas IV, and Prague Castle, the seat of government. Even after the kings had moved back up to the castle, processions took place along this route during coronation festivities.

Begin your own 'Royal Way' at the **Powder Tower** (Prašná brána), where the Royal Court once stood. Here, you can breakfast at leisure in the coffee house of the **Municipal House** (Obecní dum), an art nouveau building on Náměstí Republiky. Crossing Celetná, with its splendid Baroque facades, you will come to the **Old City Square** (Staroměstské nám).

Extensive restoration work has been in progress on this section of the Royal Way for some years and many Gothic, Baroque and Rococo buildings are already shining forth in all their former glory.

On Charles Bridge

Diagonally opposite the Church of St Nicholas on the Old City Square, you can soak up the atmosphere of the city's student life in the tiny **Café Bílý Jelinek**. From here, the path leads over the Lesser Square (Malé náměstí) to **Karlova**. This winding street zigzags past little galleries, handicrafts shops, and inns. Number 18 shelters the restaurant **U Zlatého Hada** (At the Golden Snake), the first coffee house in Prague.

After the massive Jesuit College, the Clementinum, the archway of the **Old City Bridge Tower** (Staroměstská mostecká věž) affords a view of **Charles Bridge** (Karlův most). Peter Parler, Charles IV's architect, drew up the plans for this bridge in 1342, with an eye to strategic as well as aesthetic concerns. Although the bridge seems to be a direct connection between the Old City and Hradčany, it is, in fact, built with a slight S-curve. If you stand in the middle, you'll notice that you can't see the towers of the lower-lying bridgeheads – an effect meant to disconcert intruders unfamiliar with the area.

In the course of the centuries, the bridge's broad sandstone balustrades have been decorated with statues, singly and in groups, so that today it has something of the effect of an open-air museum. And a lively museum it is. Ven-

House of the Three Violins

dors and artists offer their wares and artwork for sale, and sometimes you can find real bargains among the selection of second-hand goods. For locals and visitors alike a walk across Charles Bridge from time to time is virtually obligatory.

On the opposite bank of the Moldau, the Royal Way follows the **Mostecká**, a busy street lined with shops. Built in 1597, the **House of the Three Ostriches** (U tří pštrosů, Dražického náměstí 12, Tel: 53 61 51) – formerly the residence of the supplier of Imperial feathers – at the beginning of Mostecká is Prague's only medieval hotel, with a lovely view of the Moldau. The Mostecká runs into the **Lesser City Square** (Malostranské náměstí), where the best place for refreshment is the coffee house of the same name.

In the Apothecary Museum

The last stretch of the Royal Way leads along picturesque **Nerudova**. Many little alleyways lead off this street to the stairways, nooks and crannies, and tiny squares of the Lesser City. The **Apothecary Museum** has recently opened at No 32. Here you can view the original interior of an apothecary dating from 1821; the shop was in operation until the 1940s.

The **House of the Three Violins** (U tří housliček), easily recognised by the three violins hanging over its door, has its own tradition of fine craftsmanship; it was for generations the abode of the famous Prague violin-making family Edlinger.

The traditional path of the Bohemian kings ends at Prague Castle, reached by means of the steep stairs at the end of Nerudova. To return, you must take Line C of the underground from Hradčanská station, which brings you back to Náměstí Republiky, just by the Powder Tower where your route began.

2. In the Old City

Staré Město, the historical Old City of Prague, still has its undiscovered corners.

Hordes of people, particularly in the peak season, crowd into the busy Old City with its many cafés, restaurants, galleries and shops. Yet only a few metres away from this hubbub, dreamy, picturesque courtyards and silent alleyways slumber behind old walls, hidden to all but a few passers-by. To find this world apart and the secret routes behind its old wooden doors, you have to set out with a spirit of adventure.

Entire sections of street are linked by means of a labyrinth of back alleys and sequestered courtyards. Prague natives know how to take short-cuts through these passageways. If you've managed to find the right gateway and have escaped the bustle of the city centre, you won't long remain immune to the charms of this city within a city. The narrow alleyways and romantic courtyards house

countless small craft shops; you will find pubs with local colour or observe – and photograph – children playing and housewives at work.

A particularly interesting, example of this courtyard world is the area between **Železná** and **Jilská**. Coming from the Old City Square (Starom ěstské náměstí), turn right into the inconspicuous **Kožná**, before Celetná, and follow a narrow cobblestone street which winds past medieval shops to **Melantrichova**. On the other side of the street, a Gothic archway gives onto a large courtyard surrounded with the ruins of houses. After the next courtyard, you will come to **Michalská**.

The area's many wine cellars (*vinárna*) give you the opportunity of tasting Czechoslovakia's hearty red wine and listening in on the philosophical and political discussions of the city's students if your Czech is good enough. Even if it is not, these drinking places provide a lively insight into the life of Prague. Thus refreshed, return to the corner of the Michalská, and pass through a wooden gate on the opposite side of the street.

In the back streets of Prague

A bright sign will direct you to the next *vinárna* and a further opportunity to delve into some ancient and atmospheric back alleys where tourists are hardly ever seen. Passing through another house, traverse two more courtyards, one of which is somewhat dank and inhospitable, the other more quaint and romantic, before you reach the final wooden gate which leads you out onto the major street of **Jilská**.

Once safely back home in your hotel room, you will have a hard time reconstructing your day's route through the back streets of old Prague from a city map. Many of the alleyways in the Old City do not appear at all; it would seem that local cartographers feel that the natives of Prague ought to be able to keep a few secrets for themselves.

3. Loreto and the 'New World'

A pilgrimage – almost – to Italy, by the Hradčany Castle.

Church of the Nativity of Our Lord

Take Line A of the underground to **Hradčanská** station; a five-minute walk will bring you to **Loretánské náměstí**. An alternative to the underground is the tram: line 22 brings you to the **Památník národního písemnictví** station, from which you simply follow the footpath in the direction of Hradčany Castle.

The original Loreto is a place of pilgrimage in Italy. In the 13th century, angels are reputed to have brought the *Santa Casa*, the 'holy house' in which the Archangel Gabriel announced Jesus' birth to Mary, from the Holy Land to the Italian village of Loreto. But how, then, did Loreto come to Prague? Over the years, the Italian Loreto cult also became popular in Bohemia. Habsburg rulers found this happy legend well-suited to their purpose of bringing their heretical Hussite vassals back into the way of the true faith. They therefore set about building more than 50 replicas of the 'holy house' throughout the land; the best known and most beautiful of these is in Prague, situated directly behind the Castle.

The **Prague Loreto** is much more than just a copy of the simple little house. Between 1626 and 1750, a large complex of buildings grew up here, including a chapel, multi-storeyed cloisters, the **Church of the Nativity of Our Lord**, and an early Baroque tower with a carillon which dates back to 1694.

However, the sanctuary's main attraction is the **Loreto Treasury** (daily except Monday, 9am–noon and 1pm–5pm), which had to be built in order to accommodate the many valuable offerings – including jewelled goblets and golden robes – which have been brought to the statue of the Virgin Mary.

The Loreto Treasury

Particularly noteworthy is a monstrance weighing 12kg (26lb), set with over 6,000 diamonds. After so much splendour, the eye pauses at the monumental facade of the **Černín Palace** (Černínský Palác) just opposite. Originally, the great Italian architect Gianlorenzo Bernini was to have designed the building, but a quarrel with Count Černín prevented him – the palace was, however, built by Italian workmen and in the Italian style. Damaged in the 18th century, it has been restored more than once since then and now houses the Foreign Affairs Department.

But enough of old stories. It's time to have a look around the 'New World' – although this title is merely a translation of the street name 'Nový Svět', and the original inhabitants of this little alley off Loreto Square were once the very poorest of Hradčany's residents. Today, however, the tiny houses with their miniature windows and pocket front gardens, lovingly restored, are home to artists who hope to be discovered – particularly by wealthy tourists walking past their front doors. Number 1, the **'Golden Horn'** (U zlatého rohu), was once the residence of astronomer Johann Kepler. And you can eat well in the comfortable **Golden Pear** winery (U zlaté hrušky).

Theological Room in the Strahov Monastery library

4. Strahov Monastery

A visit to one of the most beautiful historic libraries in Europe.

Taking Line A of the underground to **Malostranská** station, you transfer to tram Line 22 or 23 and go to **Památník písemnictví**, or proceed from the underground station on foot (about 15 minutes).

Strahov Monastery (Strahovský klášter, Strahovské nádvoří 132, Prag 1, Hradčany, Tel: 53 88 41, daily except Monday 9am–5pm) sits on the slope of **Petřín Hill**. Built in 1143, the monastery shows clear traces of its long history. It burned down in 1258, and suffered damage in the Hussite War, the Thirty Years' War, a French bombardment in 1742, and occupation by the Prussian army in the centuries that followed. Additions and modifications during the Early Gothic, Renaissance, and Baroque periods have left the original Romanesque elements evident only in the **Church of the Annunciation of Our Lady**.

But Strahov is not known for unity of style; rather, for one of the most beautiful and extensive libraries in Europe. The core of the collection, which includes more than 130,000 volumes, including 2,500 first editions, was formed by an abbot. When numerous monasteries were dissolved during the secularisation that took place under Joseph II in the middle of the 18th century, the clever abbot seized his chance and purchased many valuable collections. Further additions from the libraries of defunct monasteries came after World War II.

Showpieces of the collection are the *Strahov Gospel Book* from the 10th century (a copy of this is on display; the valuable original is put away for safekeeping) and a first edition of Copernicus's *De Revolutionibus Orbium Coelestium* from 1543, in which he first put forth his heliocentric theory of the universe. As well as these rare volumes, the two ornate rooms of the library itself are impressive. Note the Baroque frescoes on the ceilings of the **Theological Room** and the small, barred cabinet containing books once banned by Church censors; also the 17th-century globe from the Netherlands.

The **Philosophical Room** is distinctive because of its richly carved and gilded walnut cabinets. Elaborate ceiling frescoes by the Rococo painter Anton Maulbertsch celebrate the accord of philosophy, science and religion. Today, the library also serves as the **Czech Literary Museum**, whose archives contain three million items, including the works of some 1,200 Czech authors.

5. Enchanting Vyšehrad

An excursion to the legendary birthplace of the Czech nation.

Vyšehrad is reached most easily by taking Line C of the underground to the station of the same name.

Legendary Vyšehrad rises up at the place where the Moldau reaches the Prague city limits. It was here, in her father's castle, that Princess Libuše had her vision of the golden city of Prague: 'I see a great city, whose fame will reach to the

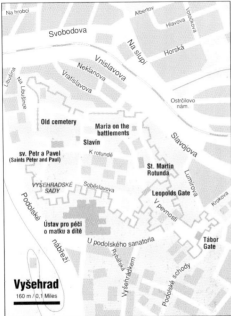

Na hrobci
Albertov
Hlavova
Votočkova
Svobodova
Na slupi
Horská
Vnislavova
Neklanova
Vratislavova
Libušina
Na Libušince
Ostrčilovo nám.
Old cemetery
Maria on the battlements
Slavín
Slavojova
sv. Petr a Pavel (Saints Peter and Paul)
K rotundě
St. Martin Rotunda
Lumírova
VYŠEHRADSKÉ SADY
Soběslavova
Leopolds Gate
Krokova
Podolské
V pevnosti
Ústav pro péči o matku a dítě
U podolského sanatoria
Tábor Gate
nábřeží
Vyšehrádkem
Rybalská
Podolské schody

Vyšehrad
160 m / 0,1 Miles

stars . . . there in the woods you shall build your castle and your settlement, which shall be named Praha.'

Contentious archaeologists maintain that this is not quite chronologically correct, as Prague Castle was built in the 9th century, while Vyšehrad was not erected until the 10th; but this has not detracted from the myth of the city's founding. The story was too attractive for composers like Smetana or Mendelssohn-Bartholdy be able to resist; they went ahead and wrote their operas *Libuše* and *Libussa's Prophecy*. All that remains of the former fortifications are a few ruins and the **Church of Saints Peter and Paul**. In the church cemetery, you can pay homage at the graves of such Czech national heroes as the composers Dvořák and Smetana and the poets Karel Hynek Mácha and Karel Čapek.

Apart from its well-tended parks, Vyšehrad itself doesn't have all that much to offer. Most people, tourists and locals alike, who get out at the underground station tend to head for the architecturally less interesting building of the **Cultural Palace**, where major rock and jazz concerts are held. Or they turn to the luxurious **Hotel Forum**, whose Pool Bar on the 25th floor commands a magnificent view of Prague.

Behind Vyšehrad stretch some of the city's less attractive more recent neighbourhoods: apartment blocks from the 1950s line up one behind the other. If you'd like to get to know this side of Prague, and perhaps sniff the air of the proletariat over beer and a card game in one of the area's few pubs, take Line C of the underground a station or two farther south, get out and wander around at will.

6. Along the Moldau

Exploring cafés and museums along the banks of the river.

Begin the day with a hearty breakfast at the **Slavia coffee house** (Národní třída 1, Tel: 26 12 40) at the beginning of Národní, or National street. The venerable coffee house is a favourite meeting-place of the Prague art scene, especially actors and actresses from the National Theatre or Nová Scéna; nor is it unknown to foreign journalists and tourists. If you're lucky enough to get a window seat with a view of the Moldau and the Lesser City, you'll want to set out on a voyage of exploration. Prague can be addictive.

The Slavia coffee house

To start with, follow the embankment Smetanovo nábřezí to the right, toward Charles Bridge. Just before the bridge, located on a little spit of land in a former water works, the **Smetana Museum** (Smetanovo muzeum, daily except Tuesday, 10am–5pm) is definitely worth a visit. On the first storey, documents and objects illustrate the life and work of Bedřich Smetana, while on the ground floor a small café would be tempting if you hadn't just had breakfast. When you've gleaned an impression of the life of this composer, who seems virtually omnipresent in Prague, look out over the Moldau's eddying waters and the streams of people moving along Charles Bridge.

A few steps will bring you to the **Square of the Knights of the Cross** (Křižovnické náměstí), often called the salon of Prague, and back into the hustle and bustle of the tourists. This square is dominated by the **Clementinum**. Despite its size, this complex of build-

ings usually goes unnoticed by most visitors and guides, whilst nearby Charles Bridge occupies everyone's attention. And yet the former Dominican monastery, which was taken over by the Jesuits in the 16th century, is excellent testimony to the way in which the spearhead of the Counter-Reformation prepared itself for the war on heresy.

A school, library, printing press and theatre demonstrate that these 'warriors' were not pedantic, single-minded dogmatists. Today, the Clementinum houses the **State Library of Czechoslovakia**, a collection which can occupy a visitor for many hours –

The Clementinum

note, for instance, the collection of globes in the Mathematics Hall (no fixed opening hours; visits by arrangement).

Next stop along your Moldau route is the Convent of St Agnes. If after visiting the Clementinum you are a bit weary and you don't want to go a further 15 minutes on foot to reach this, take tram line 17 or 133 to Náměstí Curieových, then follow Na Františku along the riverbank and turn right toward the convent.

The **Convent of St Agnes** (Anežský klášter, U milosrdných 17, Prague 1, daily except Monday, 10am–6pm) was reopened to the public in 1980 after years of restoration. Agnes was the sister of Wenceslas I and the first abbess of the Convent: she introduced the Order of the Poor Clares into Bohemia and was canonised in 1989. No traveller should miss the opportunity to visit this oldest and

Saint Agnes

Saint Agnes

most beautiful Gothic convent in Prague, part of which houses the **Museum of 19th century Czech Art**: here are displayed the work of Josef Mánes and many other notable painters of the last century. Visitors can also admire a fine selection of Bohemian glass and a permanent exhibition of applied art.

Conclude your Moldau walk on the **Botel Albatros**, located further upstream on the embankment. From the terrace café of this restaurant ship you can enjoy a refreshing drink while viewing the city of Prague and its romantic river from an entirely different angle.

7. Green Prague

Relaxing on Petřín Hill.

After Letná Park, **Petřín Hill** is the largest green space within the city of Prague. The two parks in this itinerary are located to the left and right of Hradčany Castle.

From the National Theatre, tram line 22 goes over the Moldau to **Hellichova** station (two stops) in the Lesser City. Opposite the stop, follow signs to Lanová draha, which will bring you to the cable car; now you'll have to decide whether to ascend Petřín by cable or on foot (the cable car runs daily every 20 minutes between 8am and 6pm).

If you decide to hike it (and of course this will partly depend on the weather as well as on your own level of energy), the path will lead you through fruit orchards, adorned, in the spring, with a

On the Moldau

The little 'Eiffel Tower'

wealth of blossom. The beginning of the walk is marked with a monument to the writer Jan Neruda (1834–91).

Park benches en route offer ample opportunity for rest; from these, after a few hundred metres, you can enjoy a lovely view out over Prague. Above the cable car's first stop, the terrace café of the extensive **Vinárna Nebodzizek** lures a great many visitors who are making their way up to the top; from here, too, there's a wonderful panoramic view over the opposite bank of the Moldau and Hradčany. You can also eat in this winery, but it's best to reserve a table in advance (Tel: 53 79 05, daily 11am–6pm and 7pm–11pm).

On the hill, where the cable car ends, a few sights await you: the **Maze** (Bludiště), the **Observatory** (Hvězdárna), and the **Observation Tower** (Rozhledna), a small copy of the Eiffel Tower in Paris, which has been open to the public since 1991.

After you've seen the best of the park and the city, and breathed sufficient quantities of fresh air, you must either descend to the bank of the Moldau by cable car, or wear out some more shoe leather. Several paths lead through a small wood to the foot of Petřín. If you bear to the left, you come to the grounds of the **Strahov Monastery**.

A visit to the Hill can be combined with the monastery, the **Loreto Sanctuary**, and **Hradčany**, or wandering through the picturesque alleyways of the Lesser City. You could also roam through the Court gardens **Na Valech** and **Rajská** (Paradise) in the same area, or the extensive **'Royal Garden'** (Kralovská zahrada). In order to make the latter, Ferdinand I sacrificed several vineyards in 1534; it was he who had the Royal Summer Palace built there.

Swan in Letná Park

You could then round off your visit to the Lesser City and Hradčany with a walk through **Letná Park**, which extends along the crest of a long hill to **Šverma Bridge**. A platform above the river supported a massive memorial to Stalin until 1962 and now affords good views of the city; the pavilion nearby was designed for the 1891 World Fair. Also in Letná Park you'll also find the **Sparta Stadium** and several ice-hockey rinks.

EXCURSIONS

The Castle

1. Karlštejn

To get there by car, take the E12 toward Plzen (Pilsen), Loděnice exit; or the E12 to Beroun, Srbsko-Karlštejn exit, or take Street 4 towards Dobříš, turning off before Zbraslav in the direction Dobřichovice-Karlštejn (some 35km/22 miles). By underground and train, take Metro Line B to Smíchov nádraží, then a passenger train to Karlštejn Station.

If you took the express train from Germany to Prague via Pilsen, you would know that, some 30km (19 miles) from the city, two hills suddenly shift to reveal a view of a stony cliff crowned by a castle. You might only notice it briefly – no doubt your thoughts are already in Prague at this stage in the journey – before the image vanishes from view.

Not until it's called to your attention by the tourist office's brochures would you realise that you've already glimpsed the most attractive excursion destination in the Prague area: **Karlštejn Castle** (March to December, Tuesday to Sunday 9am–4pm). From April to December each year, thousands of tourists pour into the castle. Charles IV had the structure, with its massive protective walls, built between 1348 and 1357 to protect his many religious relics and worldly treasures.

In those days, the most valuable imperial relics – a crystal container with a tooth of John the Baptist, an arm of St Anne, a golden Imperial orb, a silver sceptre and many others – were shown to the common folk once a year, on the 'Day of Relics' (the Friday after Easter), when they were honoured with a public mass. Today, too, the objects can only be seen once a year – although now the annual mass is held on 29 November, the anniversary of Charles

IV's death, in the castle's Chapel of the Holy Cross, its vaulted ceiling heavily gilded and inset with glass stars.

If you want to visit the castle, be prepared for the steep ascent on foot. But don't worry, there are plenty of distractions; the path from the little town of Karlštejn to the castle is lined with cafés, restaurants and souvenir shops.

Another option is to combine a visit to the castle with other rambles around Karlštejn. **Bohemian Karst** (Český Kras) and the **Karlštejn Forest** conceal a number of small lakes where you can picnic or paddle on a hot summer's day.

2. From Tábor to the Moldau

To Tábor, the Hussite's stronghold, and Castle Konopiště. Back to Prague along the romantic upper course of the Moldau. To get there by car, go south from Prague along the 'euroroute' E56 toward Budějovice and Linz to Tábor. Back along the E56 to Benešov and Konopiště.

The image of the God-fearing reformer and articulate opponent of ostentation and bigotry, Jan Hus, who influenced an entire epoch of Prague's history, remains oddly blurred in the city itself, obscured by other figures from the capital's rich past. In **Tábor,** however, everything is a reminder of the glory days of the Hussites.

Those well-versed in their Bibles won't have forgotten that Mount Tabor was, according to Matthew 17, verses 1–9, the site of Jesus' transfiguration. The Hussites had this in mind when in 1420, 11 years after the execution of their leader and only a few months after their Prague rebellion, thousands of them – men, women and children – came together in an enormous encampment near Castle Kozí hradek for the purpose of marching against the Imperial army and Catholic bigotry. They fortified this camp and thus the new settlement of Tábor came into being.

Tábor

From Tábor, then, began the campaign whose high points were the glorious victories at Vítkov in 1420 and Deutsch-Brod in 1422, and which, after the fall of the ingenious Field Marshal Jan Žižka in 1424, met a bitter end in the defeat near Lipany in 1434. The Hussites' dreams of a Bohemian religious nation – free of the corruption of the Catholic Church – were not to be fulfilled.

After the war, Tábor blossomed into a prosperous city, in which adherents of all faiths, including Catholics, were tolerated. The spirit of rebellion, however, remained alive, and whenever revolts against serfdom and usury broke out anywhere in Bohemia, Tabor's citizens were quick to fly their black flags emblazoned with the red goblet. Defeat at the Battle of the White Mountain in 1620 brought the city's independence to an end, and thereafter Tábor had to pay tribute to the Catholic Habsburgs.

To explore Tábor, leave the euroroute, turn right and leave your car in the car park near the castle ruins. From there, you can proceed directly to the mighty **Round Tower** and the **Bechyne Gate**, with its small historical exhibition.

Narrow, winding streets lined with run-down little houses lead up to Žižka Square, which is honeycombed, like virtually all of the city, with secret defensive passageways and military storerooms, mostly dating from the Hussite era.

Ever since the Czech Nationalist Movement proudly adopted the Hussites as their forerunners in the 19th century, a monumental **statue** of the leaders of the Hussite army has adorned this broad square. **Roland's Fountain** stands here, too, as well as two simple stone tables which were once used during the community's open-air communion.

The high tower of the **Church of the Transfiguration of Our Lord** (Chrám Promeneci Krista Pána), which dates from the Hussite era, towers over the former **Town Hall** with its splendid city arms and two-storey council room, which contains today a Museum of the Hussite movement. Nearby, an old residential home has been converted into a rustic regional restaurant, with tables on the square in summer.

A walk through Prážská ulice and the side streets off of it will lead you past studios, galleries, antique shops and bookstores. Before the City Wall, which is still quite well preserved to the north, you can see **Jordan Pond**, which was dammed for use as the city's water reservoir as early as 1492.

Although Tábor is relatively quiet, even on weekends, it seems that half of Prague, together with prams and sandwiches, gathers in the magnificent gardens and parks of **Castle Konopiště**, laid out in the 13th century.

The castle can look back on a turbulent history. Here, in 1423, in the midst of a war with the Emperor's troops, the Hussite factions negotiated about disputed liturgical questions. In the Thirty Years' War the Gothic castle was laid waste by the Swedes, to be rebuilt, later, in the Baroque style. And the Habsburg heir Archduke Franz Ferdinand – the same man whose assassination in Sarajevo in 1914 was to precipitate the outbreak of World War I – erected a stately private palace in Konopiště, which he filled with an extravagant art collection.

In the interior, the large dining room, with its tapestries depicting scenes from Cervantes' *Don Quixote*, is of particular interest. The smoking room, the library and the chapel on the second floor, as well as the countless hunting trophies in the corridors and stairways, testify to the somewhat over-polished lifestyle of the castle's master and his guests.

A part of the gigantic castle park, with its aromatic rose gardens, ponds and wildlife pens, is open to the public. There, and

Popular destination for a day-trip

also in a location at the car park, two taverns see to the visitor's physical well-being.

From Konopiště, you then proceed along a small side road east into the romantic valley of **Sázava**, and then some kilometres north towards **Jilove u Prahy**, whence a small street immediately leads off to the left, towards **Davle**. Crossing the upper Moldau by means of a bridge which seems to groan with age, you can, depending on how much time you have remaining, either drive left into the Moldau valley for a bit of spontaneous sightseeing, or take the right-hand road back to Prague.

3. Pilsner Beer in Plzeň (Pilsen)

By car, go approximately 90km (56 miles) on the A50 to Pilsen.

Beer brewing in Bohemia is a tradition dating back to the year 1082, the date of the first documented mention of brewing in Prague. However, the best Czech beer doesn't come from the capital; this title is held, incontestably, by Pilsner Source. A trip to Prague, therefore, should include a detour to this beer drinker's Mecca, only two hours' drive from the city.

Plzeň (Pilsen) has a romantic, medieval city centre, and offers, as well as many noteworthy sights, many more gastronomic options than simply beer. With the founding of the city in 1290, brewing privileges came to Plzeň; many private breweries were quick to put these to use. The **Brewing Museum** (*Pivovarské muzeum*) offers an interesting look into the history of brewing; it's housed in a Late Gothic malt-house in **Veleslavínova**, not far from the central Republic Square (Náměstí Republiky). To the east of the Old City, the street **U Prazdroje** leads to the **Source Brewery**, where the famous Pilsner beer has been produced since 1842. Enter through the imposing gateway for a tour of the premises, and sample the brew in the brewery's own pub – be careful how much you have; car-drivers should avoid alcohol altogether.

Pilsner beer is prepared like any other beer in the world: by sieving ground malt with water and hops and fermenting the mixture by adding beer yeast fungi, *saccharomyces carlsbergensis*. However, Pilsner has a unique, unmistakable flavour. This derives in part from the water used, it is unusually soft, it has a very low sodium content.

A Pilsen brewer

The malt, too – made of grain roasted in-house, with a low percentage of protein – is prepared traditionally, with particular care. The beer's characteristic flavour and strength are a result of a special mixture of first-class Saazer hops.

Another secret of Pilsner lies in its cellars, cut deep into the sandstone bedrock. Throughout the year, the cellars are kept at a uniform temperature of 1–2°C (33–35°F). The walls of the cellars, where the beer matures for two to three months, are covered with a special kind of mould, which has often been 'kidnapped' but which has never taken hold in the cellars of other breweries.

The Viennese were the first to sample beer from Plzeň, and three-quarters of the total production was already being exported abroad as early as 1865. In 1900, the legendary 'beer train' began its daily run from Plzeň to Vienna; later, a similar train went to Bremen, whence Pilsner Source was shipped to America. Currently, the annual production of the Prazdroj brewery alone amounts to 1,300,000 hectolitres (about 29 million gallons). After all this fanfare, you really must sample the brew for yourself, but please be careful: because of the beer's extremely high alcohol content, more than one person has overestimated his capacity to hold his liquor.

4. Carlsbad

If you've got the time, include a sojourn at one of the lovely spas of West Bohemia – Františkovy Lázně (Franzensbad), Mariánské Lázně (Marienbad), Jáchymov, and Karlovy Vary (Carlsbad). The latter is the best known.

Easily reached by car, train, or, in the case of Carlsbad, plane, these spas exude a demure charm and impart to the visitor a sense of now-vanished Imperial elegance. **Karlovy Vary/Carlsbad** has the longest tradition; it's here, legend has it, that Emperor Charles IV discovered the healing spring by accident while on the trail of a magnificent stag during a hunting expedition from nearby Castle

Loket. The imperial physician determined that the water had a healing effect, whereupon the Emperor, in 1349, founded a settlement which received its city charter in 1370.

At the end of the 18th century, Carlsbad became the most cosmopolitan resort in the history of the world. Crowned heads and celebrated artists alike enthused about the health-giving waters. Peter the Great came here twice – only, in theory, for the purpose of discussing Russian advances in science and culture with Leibniz – while it's documented that Goethe was here no fewer than 13 times. No other place, he said, could provide 'a more comfortable and pleasant visit'. Other resort guests included European financial magnates, who liked to stay in the 'Sanatorium Imperial'; aristo-

Carlsbad colonnade

crats, on the other hand, preferred the elegant Grand Hotel of the former baker Johann Georg Pupp. Another guest, Karl Marx, is supposed to have written several chapters of *Das Kapital* here, no doubt inspired by the presence of so many members of the exploiting classes.

Graver things have occurred in Carlsbad, as well. In 1819, the Austrian Chancellor Prince Metternich summoned the representatives of all countries he deemed trustworthy to a council at which he committed to paper the Carlsbad Decrees, a declaration of war upon all peacemaking efforts in Europe.

In earlier days, the carriage trip to Carlsbad through the narrow Valley of Teplá was dangerous; but there wasn't any shortage of parking places when the traveller arrived. Anyone trying to approach the town centre by car today had best aim for the south side of the town – you may be lucky enough to find a parking space at

The Thermal Hotel

the foot of Teplá, or directly on the embankment. By following signs to Eger, Mariánské Lázně or Prague, however, you'll be led into the modern, northern section of the town, where there's hardly any parking and from which you can't extricate yourself to drive back into the south.

Begin on the left bank of the river, notable for a row of stately buildings which include the ornate **Casino** and the huge **Grand Hotel Pupp**. The main entrance to the old Grand Hotel, which is equipped with a gorgeous lobby, a stylish tea room and an equally stylish, luxurious restaurant, is set somewhat back from the corner of Teplá. Behind the hotel, a cable car (Lanovka) carries one up the 200m (656ft) to **Friendship Heights** (Výšina Přátelství*), where an observation tower and restaurant await the visitor.You, however, continue your walk through the valley along the **Old Meadow** (Stará louka), the most expensive shopping street in the town. It's here that the glass and porcelain manufacturer **Moser**, which is based in the town, sells its world-famous vases and crockery.

On the opposite bank of the river, easily reached by any one of a number of pedestrian bridges, Viennese architects erected the renowned **Hotel Kaiserbad** shortly before the turn of the century. Next to it stands the **State Theatre**, built in 1886.

Your promenade now brings you to the **Market Square**, where a row of old-fashioned wooden stalls and the unlovely **Juri Gagarin Colonnade**, built in 1975, both darken the picture and obscure the view of the beautiful **Church of Mary Magdalene**, by K I Dientzenhofer.

After this, the **Mill Fountain Colonnade** with its pump room, the central point of this spa town, has a calming effect. There you should, if you haven't already, sample the water of one of the four springs – Vřídlo – which have made the town famous. The bathing complex further to the north isn't necessarily worth a visit; instead, walk left to the **Russian Church** (Ruský kostel). When you've put the steep ascent up **Park Street** (Savodá třída), past mighty, venerable trees and enchanting villas, behind you, you'll have a beautiful view out over the resort neighbourhood, where some 70,000 guests come for their cure each year.

Twelve springs with high mineral content, which emit some 3,000 litres (659 gallons) a minute, provide the chief ingredient of the Carlsbad cure. Vřídlo, the most famous, spouts 3 million litres (659,700 gallons) of 70°C (158°F) water every day. Drinking cures are the most important part of Carlsbad therapies, particularly in dealing with digestive complaints and chronic liver and gall-bladder diseases. If this seems too tame for you, have a sip from Carlsbad's '13th spring', as the famous *Becherovka*, Carlsbad's bitters, are also known – although their powerful effects are of dubious medicinal value.

The Grand Hotel Pupp

Carlsbad also has much to offer culturally. Rich in tradition, the annual summer film festival held here is graded 'A' in the Czech rankings, and has gained a reputation for screening the newest films from Central and Eastern Europe.

The town supports a Symphony Orchestra and stages a festival for young musicians every August, as well as a Dvořák festival in the autumn.

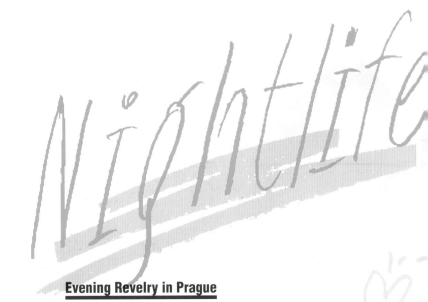

Evening Revelry in Prague

As twilight descends, a romantic veil is drawn over Prague. Illuminated by old streetlights, the city invites you to take a long stroll through its dark streets.

Small bars and cafés like the **Espresso Bar** in Karlova or the former café **U zlatého Hada** lure you in for before-dinner drinks. On the other side of venerable Charles Bridge, behind the archway in the Lesser City (Malá Strana), the **Café de Colombia**, where you can sample the herbal liqueur *Becherovka*, is usually filled to overflowing.

Offering wine, beer, and other alcoholic beverages as well as coffee, and generally open until around 11pm, the stylish coffee houses are truly comfortable. Particularly worthy of mention are the lovely art nouveau cafés **Café Slavia**, **Evropa**, **Paříž** and **U Domů**. After 7pm these venues have live classical music.

For dinner, go to a *vinárna* (wine cellar) or one of the many

Wenceslas Square at night

restaurants; but always reserve a table in advance. Otherwise you run the risk of spending your evening queueing, your empty belly growling with hunger.

As well as the many bars, coffeehouses, pubs, restaurants and wine cellars in the city centre, which are hard to overlook as you stroll around the city, Prague offers a wealth of cultural activities without equal the world over.

Walking through the city in the early evening, you can hear the sounds of organs, violins and pianos issuing from churches, old palaces and monasteries. The daily selection of classical offerings is large, and music presented in the ornate halls of historic buildings becomes not only a concert programme, but a true cultural experience. The concert hall in the **Convent of St Agnes**, or **Smetana Hall** in the Municipal House (Obcení Dům), are both worth a visit in themselves.

Many productions are also of interest to foreign visitors in the city's 25-plus theatres: **Nová Scéna** and the **National Theatre** offer opera and drama in languages other than Czech. Avant-garde pantomimes can be seen in the little **Braník Theatre** (Branické divadlo). The **Gag Theatre's** offerings are aimed directly at the funny bone. Prague is also the home of the English-Speaking Theatre, a multinational troupe. Performances in any theatre generally begin around 7pm; it is wise to reserve tickets in advance, as the majority of performances are sold out most of the time.

Prague is famous for its jazz tradition, and spontaneous performance is an integral part of this musical genre. **Reduta** is the most famous jazz club in Prague; other popular locales are the **Jazz Art Club**, the **Viola Club** in the theatre of the same name, and the **Press Jazz Club**, open until 2am. The monthly cultural programme gives detailed concert information. Posters along the city's streets also promote theatre and concert events, at somewhat shorter notice.

Culture-lovers, then, will have no problem; but things are more difficult for those who'd like to get in some dancing or to extend their night into the wee hours of the morning. In comparison with that of other European capitals, Prague's nightlife is still undeveloped. The more expensive hotels offer entertainment, ranging from dancing and cabaret to discos, to non-residents; but in general the options are limited to discos and night clubs which are rather more reminiscent of conservative dance cafés.

Jazz has a long tradition in Prague

In the summer, open-air discos on the Botels (boat hotels) **Admirál**, **Albatros** or **Racek** provide an original alternative. The larger hotels have discos which are generally more fashionable and exclusive, but ladies of the night are often in evidence seeking customers, and this can sometimes lead to misunderstandings, especially after a few drinks. In any case, you won't be allowed entry in jeans and training shoes.

The managers of the old night clubs around Wenceslas Square were quick, after liberalisation, to adjust their programmes to include striptease and similar amusements. The Hotel Ambassador's **Alhambra Club** is usually recommended, but its programme, complete with clowns, music, and variety acts, tends to be more sleep-inducing than entertaining. The same could be said of the **Jalta Club** or the **Lucerna Bar**. By contrast, **Barberina** is a relatively neutral, quite comfortable night club; here, live jazz plays, and you don't have to pay cash for human contact.

In Prague, as in every city of the former East Bloc, gambling casinos are springing up left and right. The **Hotel Forum**, the **Ambassador**, and the high-class American **Hotel Palace** have their own casinos. Anyone may enter, but there is a dress code here as well (no jeans or training shoes).

The public in such establishments includes not only the omnipresent beauties of the night, escorted by foreign businessmen or locals with foreign-currency holdings, but also curious tourists and professional gamblers. Drink prices are kept low, and the selection is extensive. In most discos, nightclubs, and casinos, you can indulge in nightlife until 4am.

Cafés and Clubs

ESPRESSO
Karlova,
Prague 1 (Staré Město).
Daily 10am–10pm.

U ZLATÉHO HADA
Karlova 18,
Prague 1 (Staré Město).
Daily 10am–11pm.

CAFÉ DE COLOMBIA
Mostecká 3,
Prague 1 (Malá Strana).
Daily 12pm–12am.

CAFE SLAVIA
Národní 1, Prague 1 (Nové Město).
Daily 10am–11pm.

CAFE EVROPA
Václavské náměstí 25,
Prague 1 (Nové Město).
Daily 10am–11pm.

CAFE PAŘIŽ
U Obecního domu 1,
Prague 1 (Staré Město,
Daily 11am–1am.

U DOMŮ
Náměstí Republiky,
Prague 1 (Nové Město).
Daily 9am–11pm.

REDUTA
Národní 20, Prague 1 (Nové Město).
Monday to Friday 8pm–2am, live
music until 12am.

JAZZ ART CLUB
Radiopalác Vinohradská 40,
Prague 1.
Daily except Monday 9pm–2am.

VIOLA CLUB
Národní, Prague 1 (Nové Město).
Saturday 8pm–12am.

PRESS JAZZ CLUB
Pařížská 9,
Prague 1 (Staré Město).
Daily except Sunday, 9pm–2am.

ALHAMBRA
Václavské náměstí 5,
Prague 1 (Nové Město).
Daily 8pm–3am.

CLUB JALTA
Václavské náměstí 45,
Prague 1 (Nové Město).
Daily except Tuesday, 9pm–4am.

LUCERNA BAR
Vodičkova 36, Prague 1 (Nové Město).
Daily 8pm–3am.

BARBERINA
Melantrichova 10,
Prague 1 (Staré Město).
Daily except Sunday, 8pm–2am.

Like so many other things in Czechoslovakia, the calendar of national holidays has been completely confused by the recent political upheavals.

Holidays which were previously associated with communist rule have simply been deleted, and replaced with new holidays, including Catholic holidays – although these are not yet officially recognised as legal.

JANUARY

New Year's Day (1st) is a holiday. **Epiphany** (6th) is also observed in many parts of the country.

Prague Winter, a music and theatre festival, is held at the beginning of January.

FEBRUARY

Carnival is celebrated early on; towards the end of the month, the **St Matthew's Festival** draws visitors to the J Fučík Park.

MARCH

Easter Monday is associated with willow-switches, bringing good luck for the coming spring.

APRIL

Jazz Praha, three days of high-quality traditional and modern jazz.
Interkamera, the international photography and audio fair in Prague.
At the end of the month so-called **witch burnings** are held in many areas, in accordance with tradition.

MAY

May Day (1st), the international workers' holiday, is a legal holiday.
Beginning of the **Prague Uprising** in 1945 is commemorated on the 5th.
The Day of Liberation from Fascism (9th), the occasion for memorial ceremonies throughout Czechoslovakia.
Prague Spring (12th), a music festival beginning on the anniversary of Smetana's death, consists of a programme of concerts and operas lasting until 4 June. **The Prague International Book Fair** begins in the middle of May.

JUNE

The Concertino Praga festival introduces up-and-coming talent.
Kmoch' Kolín, the Czech horn music festival, is held in Kolín, near Prague.
The International Film Festival is held in Carlsbad.

JULY

The **Apostles Cyril and Methodius** are honoured on 5 July.
The death of reformer **Jan Hus** is remembered on the 6th.
Prague's summer programme is enlivened by rock and pop concerts.

AUGUST

The **Intervention of 1968** is commemorated on 20 August.

SEPTEMBER

The **Vintners' Festival** in Melnik is held before the gates of Prague.
In rural regions, **harvest festivals** are celebrated.

OCTOBER

International Jazz Festival.
The **Great Pardubice Obstacle Race**, one of the most difficult horse racing events, is held. **Day of the Republic** is commemorated on the 28th.

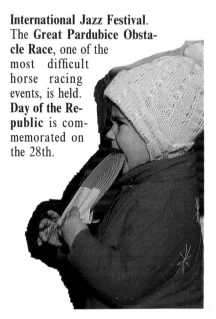

NOVEMBER

On 17 November, Prague's citizens remember the bloody suppression of the uprising in Prague's National Street, and the decisive months of 1989's **Velvet Revolution** are celebrated with processions and jubilant demonstrations, centred on Wenceslas Square.

DECEMBER

25–26 December are official Christmas holidays. Organ and choral concerts are held in Prague's churches; a festive **Christmas** mass is heard in St Vitus' Cathedral which is by Hradčany Castle (see Day 2).

Shopping

In recent decades, Prague has been known as the shopping paradise of the East Bloc. People came on weekend trips from Poland and former East Germany to shop by day and have a wild time in pubs and night clubs by night. Even before the 1989 revolution, therefore, many small shops and well-planned department stores could be found in the city centre.

Bohemian glass and tableware are valued the world over for their high quality. As such items can be bought cheaply in Prague, thanks to the advantageous rates of exchange, many visitors are ready to spend hours waiting in queues to get into the state retailing outlets. Factories are barely able to keep up with the tremendous demand.

Western tourists seem to fall prey to shopping fever and buy everything that isn't nailed down. And there's a good fundamental reason for this: things which have long sold for high prices in the West can still be had in Prague for a song. Antique dealers, however, know of the Western predilection for antiques – and their prices are accordingly high.

Galleries, meanwhile, are booming. The works of artists who were excluded from the artists' associations until 1989, in particular, are being exhibited and sold everywhere. Crafts shops, too, are doing good business. Authorised outlets offer woodcarvings from all over Czechoslovakia. 'Travelling salesmen' offer homemade items, such as marionettes or fashion jewellery, most commonly on Charles Bridge (Karlův most) or Na příkopě. Open-air markets have recently sprung up in the pedestrian zone between Republic Square (Náměstí republiky) and Wenceslas Square

(Václavské náměstí), where you can purchase everything from clothes and household goods to souvenirs and all sorts of knick-knacks.

You can also get English and German books at good prices in Prague. Since the state ceased to subsidise book publication, Czech publishers have been faced with the prospect of financial ruin, and have had to raise their prices considerably. For Prague natives,

buying books is, like so many other things, therefore hardly feasible any longer; for foreigners, on the other hand, it's quite a bargain.

Classical music fans can get good records at bargain prices; cassettes and CDs, however, are harder to find.

A typical gift to take home is Prague ham, although not many butchers offer this on a regular basis. It's easier to find a bottle of the herbal liqueur *Becherovka* or a drop of good *Slivovice*, a sort of Schnapps. And the fruity wines of Bohemia and Moldavia are not to be sneezed at.

Tuzex shops are run by the State and sell a wide range of goods duty free, but only for foreign currency (or credit cards); when shopping in them it is sensible to retain your receipts.

If you want to do some serious shopping, you'll have to reckon with long queues in large warehouses and small speciality shops alike. Especially on weekends, when locals and visitors are both out in full force, shopping becomes, in effect, a test of one's patience. The visitor is advised to shop during the week and devote his or her weekends to touring the city's many sights.

If you can't find something you particularly want in the centre of Prague, then unfortunately you can be sure it can't be found in any other part of the city.

Shops are generally open Monday–Friday 10am–6pm, Saturday 10am–2pm, closed Sunday. Warehouses have longer hours.

Glass and Porcelain

BOHEMIA MOSER
Na příkopě 12,
Prague 1.
Particularly well-made objects.

BOHEMIA
Pařížská 1,
Prague 1.
Glass, lamps, dishes.

KRYSTAL
Václavské náměste 30
(Wenceslas Square), Prague 1.

Folk Art and Crafts

ČESKA JIZBA
Karlova ulice 12,
Prague 1.

KRASNA JIZBA
Národní 36,
Prague 1.

UVA
Na příkopě 25,
Prague 1.

A+G FLORA
Přemyslovská 29,
Prague 3.
Tel: 27 17 16.
Private shop, irregular hours:
phone ahead. Clothing boutique
and gallery. According to the
owner, Prague's artists buy their
clothing here.

Haberdashery

TONAK
Celetná 30,
Prague 1.
Open daily 9am–7pm,
weekends 9am–1pm.

International Booksellers

KNIHA
Štěpánská 12 (courtyard),
Prague 1.
Open daily 9am–6pm,
weekends 9am–1pm.

KNIHA
Na příkopě 27,
Prague 1.

ZAHRANIČNI LITERATURA
Vodičkova 41,
Prague 1 (in the.Alfa Passage,
entrance Wenceslas Square).
Open daily 9am–6pm,
weekends 9am–1pm.

Jewellery

GALERIE VLASTA WASSERBAUEROVA
Staroměstské nám. 5,
Prague 1.
Unique hand-crafted items.

Fashion jewellery
Na příkopě 12, Prague 1.
Staroměstské náměstí 6
(Old City Square), Prague 1.

Department Stores
The following stores have the largest
selection of gift items, fabric, clothing, dishes, shoes, edibles, travel ac-
cessories, stationery, electric appli-
ances, books, and much more.

MAJ
Národní třída 26,
Prague 1.

KOTVA
Náměstí republiky 8,
Prague 1.

Supermarkets are located in the cellars of every department store. A particularly noteworthy delicatessen is:
POTRAVINY
Václavské náměstí 59, Prague 1.

Records
Jungmannova 20, Prague 1.
Celetná 8, Prague 1.
Václavské náměstí 17 and 51,
Prague 1.
Vodičkova 20, Prague 1.

Antiques
Můstek 3, Prague 1.
Mikulandská 7, Prague 1.
Národní trída 22, Prague 1.
Václavské náměstí 60, Prague 1.
Celetná 31, Prague 1.

69

Czech cuisine, insofar as one can speak of it as such, has Bohemian, Slovakian, and Moldavian nuances. All three are strong-flavoured, and no meal, it seems, is complete without the famous dumplings. Roast pork, or goulash with cabbage and dumplings are virtually national dishes – although these are certainly not exclusive to Czechoslovakia, as any traveller familiar with Germany and Austria knows. A well-rounded meal generally starts with soup; dessert often consists of a pudding or egg dish with a sweet sauce.

Although such fare was virtually all the visitor was offered until a short time ago, an astonishing transformation has taken place in

OUT

Prague in this regard. In the 'old Prague', menus generally offered around 200 items, of which, as a rule, only two were available; today, you can get just about anything which the spoiled Western European palate might desire, at a range of prices.

Restaurants, wine cellars (*vinárna*) and taverns (*pivnice*) which have remained under state control are divided into three distinct categories, and the diner is charged according to a fixed price scale. Second- and First-category wine cellars and restaurants can loosely be termed middle- to upper-class, while the pubs and inns of the Third category lean more towards the rustic.

For any eatery, in any category, state or private, it is advisable to book a table well in advance.

Prague's **coffee houses** can look back on a long history and tradition; since 1989, they've breathed anew the typical atmosphere one associates with such cafés. **Slavia**, **Paříž** and **Evropa** (see the *Nightlife* section for addresses of these establishments) are particularly worthy of mention in this context. Coffee house menus generally offer lighter meals and snacks; to drink, you can order almost anything except beer.

Stand-up snack bars, or 'buffets', have become an open-air alternative to the prohibitive cost of dining in a restaurant for many Prague residents. Open from 7am–6pm, they're just the thing for a not-too-costly bite to eat – provided you aren't a vegetarian. In addition, for food-on-the-hoof addicts many squares and streets have developed a true fast-food cuisine through their hot-dog and waffle stands.

Prague's **taverns** are made for drinking beer. Statistics show that

every inhabitant of the golden city on the Moldau puts away 150 litres (40 gallons) of beer (*pivo*) each year; and he doesn't, in general, tipple in the privacy of his own home, but rather in one of the hopelessly over-crowded venues.

Some of the city's more than 1,500 taverns can look back on several centuries of history. Such places are the focus of Prague's social and political life. Under the communist regime, they were the only place where one could discuss political alternatives more or less freely, and wax philosophical. Here, people tell stories, complain, laugh – and drink. Patrons are a mixed lot: students, intellectuals, and workers mingle with one another and, not infrequently, with groups of foreign visitors. Uninhibited, people sit pressed closely together on long wooden benches, and conversations can quickly develop between tourists and locals provided they have a language in common.

In the historic taverns, of course, you won't meet many locals. Such places tend to be the stamping-ground of organised tourism. In the old favourite **U Fleků** (Křemencova 9, Prague 1, Tel: 29 32 46, open daily 8.30am–11pm), one of the oldest in Prague, townspeople quietly retreat in the afternoon and evening to let the field be taken over by hordes of tourists hungry for adventure and thirsty for beer. At these times, the polyglot waiters work like Trojans. The pub, which has seats for 960 guests under its ceiling's Gothic vaulting and in its garden, serves 6,000 hectolitres (158,500 gallons) of its dark, home-brewed beer every year, while cabaret and live music entertain its guests.

Things aren't much different in **U Svatého Tomáše** (Letenská 12, Prague 1, Tel: 53 00 64, open daily 11am–12am), in the vaulted cellars of the former monastery brewery. Indeed, there are many historic inns with their own breweries in Prague. The stories of how these came into being are recounted in well-loved, well-known anecdotes: for example, in 1843, the carter Salzmann met the tailor Pinkas, and let him taste some Pilsener beer. The tailor found the brew so good that he immediately changed his profession and opened a bar. And therefore Pilsener beer is still served today in **U Pinkasů** (Jungmannovno náměstí 15, Prague 1, Tel: 26 18 04, open daily 7am–3pm and 4pm–12am). **U Kalicha** (Na bojisti 12, Prague

2, Tel: 29 60 17, open 11am–3pm and 6pm–11pm) came to fame through the story of *The Good Soldier Schwejk.*

Pubs which are less well-known to tourists and more authentically local are **U Medvídků** (Na Perštýně 7, Prague 1, Tel: 235 89 04, open 9am–11pm) and **U Schnellů** (Tomášská 12, Prague 1, Tel: 53 29 94, open from 11am–3pm and 4.30pm–12am).

The two vaulted rooms of the pub **U Kocoura** (Nerudova 2, Prague 1, Tel: 53 89 62) are designated smokers' and non-smokers' rooms, a pleasant consideration for those diners who would like to enjoy their hearty pork roasts and *pivo* without the interference of clouds of smoke. Most of these pubs serve straightforward food, as well as beer: common dishes are, as one might expect, roast beef and pork with sauerkraut and dumplings, goulash, and, occasionally, venison. Last orders for drinks is 11pm in small *pivnice* and major pubs alike.

Restaurants in Prague don't limit their lunch and dinner offerings to low-budget roast meats or goulash as do the pubs and wine cellars. The following listings include a few of the new eating alternatives which have already cropped up elsewhere in the itineraries of this book. As privatisation continues in the field of gastronomy, the selection should grow as the years go by, and the quality should rapidly improve. There are already restaurants specializing in Bulgarian, Chinese, German, Italian, Indian, Jewish, Russian and Vietnamese cuisine in the capital, and new restaurants and eating places are opening all the time to cater for the recent influx of tourists and businessmen.

Solid Bohemian Fare

PELIKAN
Na příkopě 7,
Prague 1.
Tel: 22 07 82.
Daily 11am–11.30pm.

PIVNICE SKOŘEPKA
Skořepka 1,
Prague 1.
Tel: 22 80 81.
Daily 11am–11pm, Saturday until 8pm. Speciality: grilled knuckle of pork.

U PAVLICE
Fügnerovo náměstí 1,
Prague 2.
Tel: 29 03 73.
Weekdays 4pm–11pm.
Old Czech home cooking.

U ZLATÉHO SOUDKU
Ostrovní 28,
Prague 1.
Tel: 20 37 78.
Weekdays 11am–10pm. Speciality: duck with cabbage and dumplings.

Krušovicka Pivnice
Široká 20,
Prague 1.
Tel: 231 66 89.
Daily 12pm–12am.

Refined Dining

Gourmets will perhaps be less than appreciative of the Czech cuisine, particularly if confronted with it twice a day. However you don't need an especially full wallet to eat differently (main courses cost start at around £3.50/$7), but don't forget to reserve a table in advance.

Vinárna (Wine Cellars)

U Sedmi Andělů
Jilská 20,
Prague 1.
   Tel: 26 63 55.

Daily except Sunday, 12pm–3pm and 6pm–12am.
Attentive service, old-style interior.

U Plebana
Betlemské náměstí 8,
Prague 1.
Tel: 26 52 23.
Daily except Sunday, 12pm–3pm and 6pm–12am.
Elegant appetisers and a tasty breast of duck.

U Sixtů
Celetná 2,
Prague 1.
Tel: 236 79 80.
Daily from 12pm–1am.
High-class dining in gorgeous vaulted cellars.

U Zlaté Studny
Karlova 5,
Prague 1.
Tel: 26 33 02.
Daily 11am–3pm and 5pm–12am.
Moravian wine and specialities.

Opera Grill
Karolíny Světlé 35,
Prague 1.
Tel: 25 55 08.
Weekdays 7pm–2am.
The best international cuisine the city can offer with authentic, old-fashioned decor.

U Markyze
Nekázanka 8,
Prague 1.
Tel: 22 42 89.
Monday to Saturday, 7pm–3am.
Bohemian cuisine with many antiques on display.

Non-Bohemian

Vegetarians will have trouble finding something to eat in this city on the Moldau. Some 'foreign' restaurants offer a few vegetarian dishes (with Czech overtones), of which these are the most recommendable:

RESTAURANT THANG LONG
Dukelských hrdinů 48,
Prague 7.
Tel: 80 65 41.
Daily 12pm–3pm and 5pm–12am.
Vietnamese cuisine.

RESTAURANT ASIE
Letohradská 50,
Prague 7.
Tel: 37 02 15.
Weekdays 11am–11pm.
Asian cuisine.

HOTEL PALACE
Panská 12,
Prague 1.
Tel: 235 93 84.
Daily 11am–10pm.
Hotel bistro with salad bar and rice dishes.

ČINSKA RESTAURANT
Vodičkova 19,
Prague 1.
Tel: 26 26 97.
Daily except Sunday 12pm–3pm and 6pm–11pm.
Chinese cooking.

TRATTORIA VIOLA
Národní 7,
Prague 1.
Tel: 26 67 32.
Daily 11.30am–3pm and 5.30pm–11pm, closed at weekends in July and August.
Italian cuisine; the many vegetable and salad dishes on the menu are, alas, not often actually available.

RESTAURANT PEKING
Legerova 64,
Prague 2.
Tel: 29 35 31.
Daily except Sunday 11.30am–3pm and 5.30pm–11pm.
Chinese cuisine; authentic dishes served in large portions.

Practical Information

By Car

Drivers need a national driving license, registration papers, and a sticker on their car showing country of origin.

You can only find unleaded fuel at a few petrol stations, but it's certainly available in Prague. Currently, a litre costs about 18 crowns, a little less than 50p/$1. The petrol tokens which were formerly customary have been abolished; tourists, like all the other drivers, have to wait in line at the pumps and pay in crowns.

Speed limits are 60km/h (38mph) in residential areas, 110km/h (68mph) on motorways, and 90km/h (56mph) on country roads. Speeding is punishable with monetary fines of some 160 crowns. Don't underestimate the numerous speed traps. Alcohol is completely forbidden to drivers in Czechoslovakia.

Main border crossings from Germany: Zittau-Hrádek n. Nisou, Seifhennerdorf-Warnsdorf, Schmilka-Hřensko, Bahrtal-Petrovice, Altenberg-Cínovec, Reitzhein-Horn Sv. Sebastiána, Oberwiesenthal-Boží Dar, Bad Brambach-Vojtanov, Waldmünchen-Liskova, Schachten-Všeruby, Selb-Aš, Schirnding-Pomezí, Waidhaus-Rozvadov, Furth im Wald-Folmava, Bayrisch Eisenstein-Železná Ruda, Phillipsreut-Strážný.

Main border crossings from Austria: Wollowitz-Dolní Dvořište, Gmünd-České Velenice, Neu Nagelberg-Halamky, Grametten-Nová Bystrice, Dobersberg-Slavonice, Drosendorf-Vratěnín, Mitter Retzbach-Hnanice, Kleinhaugsdorf-Hatě, Drasenhofen-Mikulov, Reinthal-Poštorná, Kittsee-Jarovce.

Until recently many such border crossings were restricted to German, Austrian and Chzechoslovakian vehicles. These restrictions, however, have been lifted and now all border cross-

ings are open to all vehicles from other nationalities.

By Train

There are direct trains to Prague from Stuttgart and Munich (an 8-hour trip), Frankfurt (10 hours), Berlin (6 hours), Hamburg (10 hours), and Vienna (6 hours).

ČSFR RAILWAYS (ČSD)
Kaiserstrasse 63,
W6000 Frankfurt/Main.
Tel: Frankfurt (069) 23 45 67

By Plane

Prague, Czechoslovakia's only international airport, has direct flights from London, New York, Frankfurt/Main, Cologne/Bonn, Munich, Hamburg, Zurich, Geneva, Vienna, Montreal and Toronto. You can get detailed flight information from the Czech airline ČSA, which has offices in many major cities.

By Bus

There are a great many different bus tours to Czechoslovakia which include overnights from Germany, Austria or Italy. From Germany, you can book organised tours from:
DEUTSCHE TOURING
Am Römerhof 17, D6000 Frankfurt 1.
Tel: Frankfurt (069) 790 32 48.

By Boat

Groups or individuals can sail into Czechoslovakia along the Elbe by boat or ship from Schmilke-Hrensko, or along the Danube from Bratislava. Ask your local travel agent for details.

Visas

Citizens of the EC and US need a passport, but no longer require a visa, for stays of up to 90 days in Czechoslovakia. Citizens of Canada,

however, still need visas to enter the country.

TRAVEL ESSENTIALS

Customs

Import: the following personal items can be brought into the country duty-free: 250 cigarettes or 50 cigars or 250g (9oz) of tobacco, 2 litres of wine, 5 litres of beer, 1 litre of spirits (tobacco and alcohol only permitted to persons over 18 years of age), up to 1kg (2lbs) of chocolate and chocolate products, and gifts (Czech citizens up to 3,000 crowns, foreigners up to 1,000 crowns in value).

Edibles, fruit and flowers may only be brought in only for personal use. However, visitors are permitted to bring in 1000 rounds of ammunition for hunting weapons.

Export: you may take gifts totalling 500 crowns in value out of the country. Exempt from this limit are articles purchased in a Tuzex hard currency shop or purchased with a credit card. Save all receipts. Most consumer goods, particularly groceries and household items, cannot be taken out of the country. When entering the country, enquire about the specific regulations and changes.

Animals: dog and cat owners must show a certificate of inoculation between 3 days and 3 weeks old.

Electricity

Czechoslovakian outlets are 220 Volts; in a few rare cases 120-Volt outlets are also available.

Climate

Warm, rainy summers and long dry winters are typical of Czechoslovakia's Continental climate. Prague receives some 476mm (18.5in) of rainfall per year.

Tipping

In general, a service charge is included in the bill. However, it is customary to round up the sum when paying. Because prices are so cheap, satisfied foreign customers may be inclined to give the waiter more than the 10 per cent service charge; local diners, however, will probably not follow this practice.

Currency

Czech crowns (Koruna or Kčs) circulate in banknotes of 10, 20, 50, 100, 500 and 1000 crowns; the coins are for 1, 2, 5 and 100 crowns. Eurocheques and credit cards are accepted. You can change money in the larger hotels, exchange offices and banks. Exchange offices and travel agencies are open weekdays until about 9pm.

'Black market' exchange is illegal, and hardly worthwhile in any case. The flourishing black market of earlier days has come to an almost total halt on account of today's currency policies. In Czechoslovakia as in other reforming countries of Eastern Europe, the black market only serves to encourage organised crime, hindering the reform efforts of the new democratic government, which relies on a steady foreign-currency economy. Bringing crowns into or out of the country is prohibited.

GEOPOLITICAL INFORMATION

Politics and Economy

Czechoslovakia is a federation formed of the Czech and Slovakian republics, each of which has its own government and legal system. The central government in Prague, however, has the right of veto at any time. The 1989 revolution has helped to reawaken the old hostilities between the two republics. A strong political movement in Slovakia has as its ultimate goal the complete independence of the republic.

The government which replaced the communist rulers after the 'Velvet Revolution' of 1989 has not yet had time tangibly to improve conditions in the country. The shift to democracy was based on the elections in June 1990, the country's first free elections in over 42 years. The Citizens' Forum candidates received the majority, followed by the Christian Democrats. The Communists got 13 per cent of the vote. The current President of Czechoslovakia is the dramatist and writer Václav Havel.

The privatisation of state property has been going on since 1990, and state-held businesses are being sold to private investors and stock companies in the course of what is termed Small and Large privatisation. Foreign investors, too, are being encouraged to bring in their money with high legal protection and advantageous tax laws. Despite the sharply rising prices and the absence of comparable wage increases, a majority of citizens support the reforms.

Geography and Population

Prague is the capital of the Czechoslovakian Federal Republic, and is situated at latitude 50°8'N and longitude 14°32'E. Czechoslovakia's 15.5 million inhabitants – 1.2 million of whom dwell in Prague – are 64 per cent Czech and 30 per cent Slovak. German, Hungarian, Polish, and Ukrainian minorities make up the remaining 6 per cent.

Since the revolution, chapels and churches throughout the country have been undergoing major restauration. Roman Catholicism is the strongest of the 18 recognised faiths, especially in Slovakia; Bohemia, on the other hand, remains more Protestant, even Hussite. Recently, particularly among the younger set, non-Christian religions have begun to attract more adherents.

Business Hours

Most shops are open from 9am–9pm; certain specialised shops from 10am–6pm. Many smaller shops close for two hours at midday. On Saturday, stores close between noon and 1pm; the large department stores, however, are an exception, staying open until 6pm.

Banks are open Monday to Friday 8am–12pm; larger branches remain open until 5pm.

Exchange offices work from 8am until at least 7pm each day; some remain open until 10pm. For a slightly higher commission, you can exchange money at the larger hotels around the clock.

Public Holidays

1 January New Year's Day.
Easter Monday
1 May May Day/Workers' Day.
8 May End of World War II.
28 October Founding of Czechoslovakia (1918).
17 November Revolution Day.
25–6 December Christmas.

Religious holidays such as Corpus Christi and Assumption are celebrated in many areas, but are not yet acknowledged legal holidays.

Print

Foreign periodicals can be found at hotel kiosks and in some bookshops. Recently English and German weekly papers, published in Czechoslovakia, have also begun appearing in Prague. You can find programmes of events, restaurant guides, and information brochures in tourist offices.

English, French, Russian and German books are readily available in Prague at any of several international booksellers.

Broadcasting
Radio and television stations are still state-run institutions. **Channel 4** of the state radio (MW/AM255) broadcasts a programme of entertainment and information in English and German. **Radio 1,** its frequency still variable, is one of the first private radio stations in Czechoslovakia; it's organised and moderated by young Prague citizens. The state television station **OK 3** has broadcast programmes in English, German and French since 1990.

Post
Stamps can usually be bought wherever postcards are sold. Ask about prices for letters and postcards when you get to the country, as postal rates are continually rising.

The red mailboxes can be seen everywhere. Larger post offices are open Monday to Friday 8am–7pm, Saturday 8am–12pm; smaller branches are only open Monday to Friday 8am–1pm or 3pm. The main post office is located at Jindřišská 14, Prague 1, Tel: 26 48 41.

Telephone, Telex and Fax
There are two different models of telephone in Czechoslovakia – if they work. One kind takes one-crown coins and can only be used for local calls. The other will also take two- and five-crown coins, but is only of limited suitability for foreign calls. If you want to call abroad, your best bet is to go to a post office or hotel; the latter, of course, add a surcharge of between 20 and 30 per cent.

In most major hotels, you can receive or send a fax or telex. First-class hotels, furthermore, generally make office services available to their guests, so that you can also have access to computers and printers.

EMERGENCIES

Medical Assistance
Emergencies are treated in every city clinic. Treatment and hospital attention have to be paid for in foreign currency, but medicine must be paid for in crowns.

Emergency	155
Ambulance	37 33 33
Dental Emergency Service	374
Fire	150
Police	158

Chemists' shops are open during normal business hours and have information and addresses for emergency services.

Breakdown Service
Although there is an organised breakdown service with over 31 branches in Czechoslovakia, it doesn't often stock spare parts for foreign cars. It's therefore a good idea to arrange for coverage from your own country's automobile club. Open 24 hours, the central office of the breakdown service is in Prague at Limuzská 12a, Tel: 02 154 or 773 45 53.

Personal Safety

In comparison with Western European countries, Czechoslovakia has a relatively low crime rate. Since 1990, however, such misdemeanours as theft, swindling and pick-pocketing have increased considerably.

Leave valuables in your hotel safe, and park your car in a supervised car park or garage.

If you should lose all your money or identification papers, apply to your country's consulate for assistance.

GETTING AROUND

Public Transport

You can buy tickets for public transportation at kiosks and automatic vending machines. In buses and trams, you must cancel a new ticket every time you change vehicles. In the underground, you can transfer as often as you wish within a period of 90 minutes. A ticket costs 4 crowns at the time of going to press; children and pensioners ride free.

Buses link the suburbs and the city centre, or service longer routes. For detailed information about local or foreign connections, contact Florenc Bus Station in Prague, Tel: 22 14 45.

The Prague **underground** is a quick and convenient way to get around. You can reach all of Prague's major sights with the three lines, and it's easy to transfer from one to another. Underground stations are marked with a large 'M'. Service begins at 5am and ends at midnight. For tourists, the 24-hour ticket, which costs a mere 8 crowns, is a bargain.

Trams in this city are slow and old-fashioned, but offer a good way to get to see something of Prague during your ride (particularly Line 22, which runs past many highlights).

After midnight, **taxis** are the only way to get anywhere in Prague, apart from a few night bus routes. There are plenty of taxi stands in the city centre and in front of the large hotels. Be firm and make the driver switch on the meter, otherwise you could be ripped off. You can recognise official taxis by their taxi plates and the licence number in the interior. Taxis can be ordered by calling 20 39 41 or 20 29 51.

Many taxi drivers will be happy to drive you around Prague and its environs for a half or whole day. If you've made sure that the car is in working order, the driver knows his way around and perhaps has a little English, go ahead and try to agree on a reasonable price (£25–30/ $50–60 for a whole day in a Mercedes, for example).

Driving Yourself

Safety belts are required when driving in Czechoslovakia. Traffic regulations are hardly different from any other European country, but be particularly careful not to drink before driving. Take note of no-parking zones, as the police are generous with parking tickets.

You may notice that the locals generally take off their windscreen wipers and even their fog lights if they're planning to leave their car parked for a long time – unfortunately not without reason. If you're in Czechoslovakia with your own highly-prized car, it's wise to leave it in a supervised parking area.

Car Rental

You can rent Hertz, Avis and Europcar vehicles from Pragocar in Prague (credit cards accepted), providing you can present a valid national driver's licence. A standard passenger car will cost about £20/$40 a day, with unlimited mileage. For further information, contact:

PRAGOCAR
Stěpánská 42, Prague 1.
Tel: 02-235 28 25, Telex: 12 26 41.

The **Hotel Inter-Continental** also rents cars. You can reserve by calling 02-231 95 95.

LEAVING THE CITY

Domestic Flights

From Prague, you can reach Brno, Bratislava, Karlovy Vary, Košice, Ostrava, Sliac, Piešťany and Tatry-Poprad by plane. ČSA (the national airline representatives) can give information about other connections. Foreigners must pay for domestic flights in Western currency.

By Train

The entire country is accessible by train, at a relatively cheap price. Fare and scheduling information are available 24 hours a day in Prague on 02-26 49 30/236 05 65; also on 02-234 from 7am–3pm Monday to Friday.

You can get train tickets at the Prague Railway Station, payable in crowns. International seat or couchette reservations, however, must be paid for in foreign currency; you can get these from the **Čedok** office at Na příkopě 18, Prague 1. Unfortunately, to do so you'll have to queue up in the morning until noon (don't forget your passport and money!), and you won't be able to pick up your tickets until the following day – after queuing once again.

If you'd rather not go through this rigmarole, try one of the many local travel agencies.

Boat Trips

In peak season (1 May to 15 October), very popular sight-seeing tours along the Moldau depart from Prague. Call 29 38 03 for detailed information, or ask at the departure quay, Prague 2, Nábřezí B Engelse at the Palacký Bridge in the harbour, tel: 29 83 09.

ACCOMMODATION

Hotels and Private Rooms

Reserving a hotel room in Prague during the peak season can be a hopeless endeavour. Many hotels have fixed contracts with foreign travel agencies, which means that a reservation for a single traveller can only be accepted at very short notice; a hotel cannot accommodate its major cus-

tomers if too many single beds have been reserved in advance.

One alternative is to book through a travel agency or the Čedok office, which has a number of rooms in various hotels at its disposal. However, the hotels you book in this way won't be much of a bargain.

Another option is a private room. Many agencies rent out rooms in the centre of Prague, starting at around £8/$15 per person per day. These can also be rented at short notice. As well as the state agencies **Čedok** and **Pragotours**, **Büro Hello** (Gorkého-Senovázné nám. 3, Prague 1, Tel: 222 42 83) generally gets results.

Exclusive and 5-Star Hotels

HOTEL PALACE
Panská 12, Prague 1.
Tel: 235 93 94.

HOTEL INTER-CONTINENTAL
Náměstí Curieovych, Prague 1.
Tel: 231 18 12.

INTERHOTEL ESPLANADE
Washingtonova 19, Prague 1.
Tel: 22 60 56.

INTERHOTEL AMBASSADOR
Václavské náměstí 5, Prague 1.
Tel: 22 33 55.

HOTEL FORUM
Kongresová 1, Prague 4.
Tel: 41 01 11.

HOTEL PANORAMA
Milevská 7, Prague 4.
Tel: 41 61 11.

Mid-Range Hotels

HOTEL ATLANTIC
Na Poříči 9, Prague 1.
Tel: 231 85 12.

HOTEL EVROPA
Václavské náměstí 29, Prague 1.
Tel: 236 52 74.

Simple Hotels

HOTEL KORUNA
Opatovická 16, Prague 1.
Tel: 29 39 33.

HOTEL CENTRAL
Rybná 8, Prague 1.
Tel: 232 42 40.

HOTEL ADRIA
Václavské náměstí 26, Prague 1.
Tel: 235 28 85.

Botels (boat hotels)

Floating hotels on the Moldau can be an unusual experience. There are two of these in the capital. A double room

with shower costs about £25/$50. You can reserve through the Čedok office.

BOTEL ALBATROS
Nábřeží L Svobody, Prague 1.
Tel: 231 36 34.

BOTEL ADMIRAL
Horejsí nábřeží, Prague 5.
Tel: 54 74 45.

Youth Hostels

For information about youth hostels and student dormitories, where students and young people can stay in summer for about £1.50/$3 a night, contact the **CKM** office, Zitná 26, Prague 2, Tel: 02-236 66 40.

CULTURE

Museums

In view of the fact that Prague itself is something like a large open-air museum, travellers who only have a few days to spend in the city aren't usually inclined to enter a museum during their visit. However, in case you are in the mood to do so – after all, you might have a rainy afternoon – here are the contours of Prague's extensive museum landscape.

NATIONAL MUSEUM
Václavské náměstí 68, Prague 1.
Daily except Tuesday 9am–4pm, Saturday and Sunday until 5pm.

ANTONIN DVOŘAK MUSEUM
Ke Karlovu 20, Prague 2.
Daily except Monday 10am–5pm.

STRAHOV MONASTERY
(STRAHOVSKY KLAŠTER)
Strahovské nádvoří 132, Prague 1 (Hradčany).
Daily except Monday, 9am–5pm.
See itinerary on 'Strahov Monastery' see page 45.

SCHWARZENBERG PALACE MILITARY MUSEUM
Hradčanské náměstí,
Prague 1 (Hradčany).
May to October, Monday to Friday 9am–3.30pm, Saturday and Sunday 9am–5pm.
The military museum displays everything from crossbows to swords of various epochs.

MOZART MUSEUM (MUZEUM ČESKÉ HUDBY, EXPOZICE MOZARTA)
Mozartova 15, Prague 5 (Smíchov).
Daily except Tuesday 10am–5pm.

MUZEUM HLAVNIHO MĚSTA PRAHY
Nové Sady J Švermy (City Park),
Prague 8 (Karlín).
Daily except Monday 10am–5pm.
History of Prague, with a model of the city 150 years ago.

MUSICAL INSTRUMENT MUSEUM
(MUZEUM HUDEBNICH NASTROJŮ)
Lázenska 2, Prague 1.
Saturday and Sunday 10am–12pm and 2pm–5pm.

NAPRSTKOVO MUZEUM
Betlemské náměstí 1, Prague 1.
Daily except Monday, 10am–6pm.
Naprstek and other explorers collected this ethnographic collection from Asia, Africa and America.

The **National Gallery** consists of 7 collections in different buildings:

1 & 2 ŠTERNBERSKY PALAC
Hradčanské náměstí, Prague 1.
Daily except Monday 10am–6pm.
European Old Masters. Nineteenth and 20th century French art.

3 JIŘSKY KLAŠTER
(ST GEORGE MONASTERY)
Nam U sv Jiri, Burgareal,
Prague 1 (Hradčany).

Daily except Monday 10am–6pm.
Old Masters, including 14th-century painters Vysebrdsky and Trebonsky.

4 GALERIE MODERNIHO UMĚNI
Dukelských hrdinů 47,
Prague 7 (Holešovice).
Daily except Monday 10am–5pm.
Modern Czech art. This gallery provides long-awaited exhibition space for artists such as Preisler, Mucha, Čapek, Kupka, Kubista and many others. Contemporary painters banned from the artists' societies before the 'Velvet Revolution' of 1989 are also to be exhibited here.

5 PALAC KINSKYCH (KINSKY PALACE)
Staromřestské náměstí 12, Prague 1.
Daily except Monday 9.30am–5pm.
Drawing collection.

6 ZBRASLAV CASTLE
In the town of the same name, 15km (9¼ miles) southwest of Prague on Country Road 4.
April to November daily except Monday 10am–6pm.
Collection of Czech sculpture from the 19th and 20th centuries.

7 CONVENT OF ST AGNES
U milosrdných 17, Prague 1.
Daily except Monday 10am–6pm.
19th-century Czech painting. The beautifully-restored monastery is a fitting setting for art which is so closely bound up with the rebirth of the Czech national spirit.

POSTAL MUSEUM
(POŠTOVNI MUZEUM)
Holečkova 10, Prague 5.
Daily except Monday 10am–5pm.

RUDOLF COLLECTION
Hradčany (Second Castle Courtyard), Prague 1.
Daily except Monday 10am–6pm.

In the 16th century, Rudolf II's collections were some of the largest and most valuable of their time. Today, gems by the painters Titian, Rubens and Brandl are among the offerings on display.

SMETANA MUSEUM
Novotného lávka 1, Prague 1.
Daily except Tuesday 10am–5pm.

NATIONAL TECHNICAL MUSEUM
(NARODNI TECHNICKÉ MUZEUM)
Kostelní 42, Prague 7.
Daily except Monday 9am–5pm.

STATE JEWISH MUSEUM
Jáchymova 3, Prague 1.
Daily except Monday 9.30am–5pm.

Theatre
Exact dates and times for performances should be available from the tourist office. Information about who is playing what where can also be gleaned from posters along the street.

Weekly and monthly magazines in Prague print calendars of events.

Prague's theatres offer the foreign visitor many options including clowns, pantomime, 'black theatre', rock and jazz.

The multi-screen theatre *Laterna Magika* in the **Nová Scéna** has been popular, particularly with visitors, for decades; films and slides are projected onto different screens at various heights, while live actors perform on the stage. Prague director Alfred Radok first introduced his multivision concept at the World Exhibition in Brussels in 1958.

A whole new theatre experience in Prague is the English Theatre. A young troupe of American, German and Czech artists present new stagings of dramatic classics. Still without its own permanent house, the company plays in different theatres around the city; posters give programme information.

Major Venues

NARODNI DIVADLO
(NATIONAL THEATRE)
Národní 2, Prague 1.
Tel: 20 43 41.

NOVA SCÉNA (LATERNA MAGIKA)
Národní 4, Prague 1.
Tel: 20 62 60.

SMETANOVO DIVADLO
(OPERA HOUSE OF THE NATIONAL THEATRE)
Vítězného února 8, Prague 1.
Tel: 26 97 46.

TYLOVO DIVADLO
(NATIONAL THEATRE STAGE)
Železná 11, Prague 1.
Tel: 22 72 81.

ROKOKO DIVADLO
Václavaské náměstí 38, Prague 1.
Tel: 235 29 22.

REDUTA
Národní 20, Prague 1.
Tel: 20 38 25.
Jazz, rock concerts, modern theatre.

GAG DIVADLO
Národní 25, Prague 1.
Tel: 26 54 36.
Pantomime, art school.

ENGLISH-SPEAKING THEATRE
*Václavské Náměstí 28
(Alfa Arcade), Prague 1.*
Tel: 26 14 49.

ŠPEIBL A HURVINEK
Římská 45, Prague 1.
Tel: 25 16 66.
Puppet theatre.

DIVADLO PANTOMIMY –
BRANIK
*Branícká ulice 63,
Prague 4 (Braník).*
Tel: 46 05 07.
Avant-garde, pantomime.

DIVADLO NA ZABRADLI
*Aneneské náměstí 5,
Prague 1.*
Tel: 236 04 49.
Pantomime.

Tickets

You can book tickets for concerts and opera in the major houses through foreign travel agencies before you get to Prague. Tickets are also available in ticket offices, agencies, hotels and tourist information offices.

Prague Art Nouveau

Even before the turn of the century, magnificent art nouveau houses were built in Prague.

One of the purest examples is the so-called **Peterka House** (No 777) on Wenceslas Square. The Czech architect Jan Kotěra completed this residential building in a single year (1899–1900).

Also on Wenceslas Square, the famous **Hotel Evropa**

was built in 1904. Today, it often serves as a set for international films, as well as an attraction for thousands of tourists. The plant reliefs typical of the style are particularly well-executed here.

Prague Railway Station, an art nouveau complex dating from 1909, is a happy example of modernisation. The building was expanded in the 1970s without damage to the structure and line of the original station.

The best-known art nouveau building in Prague is the **Municipal House** on Republic Square. You can combine a visit to this house, with its magnificent details, mosaics, and chandeliers, wrought-iron and wood panelling, with a stop at the coffee house or restaurant inside. Most 'Prague Spring' festival concerts take place here, in the Smetana Hall.

USEFUL ADDRESSES

Embassies and Consulates

Austria
Viktora Huga 10, Prague 5.
Tel: 54 65 57 or 54 65 50.

Canada
Mickiewitzova 6,
Prague 6.
Tel: 32 69 41.

France
Velkopřevorské
náměstí 2,
Prague 1.
Tel: 53 30 42.

Germany
Vlašská 19,
Prague 1.
Tel: 53 23 51.

Great Britain
Thunovská 14,
Prague 1.
Tel: 53 33 47.

Italy
Nerudova 20,
Prague 1.
Tel: 53 06 66.

Netherlands
Maltézske náměstí 1,
Prague 1.
Tel: 53 13 78 or
53 13 68.

Switzerland
Pevnostní 7,
Prague 6.
Tel: 32 04 06 or 32 83 19.

USA
Tržiště 15,
Prague 1.
Tel: 53 66 41.

The Municipal House

Airlines

AEROFLOT
Na příkopě 15, Prague 1.
Tel: 26 08 62 or 36 78 15 (airport).

AIR FRANCE
Václavské náměstí 10, Prague 1.
Tel: 26 01 55 or 36 78 19 (airport).

AIR INDIA
Václavské náměstí 15, Prague 1.
Tel: 22 38 54.

ALITALIA
Revolucní 5, Prague 1.
Tel: 231 05 35.

AVA
Parižká 1, Prague 1.
Tel: 231 64 69 or 36 78 18 (airport).

BRITISH AIRWAYS
Stepánská 63, Prague 1.
Tel: 236 03 53.

KLM
Václavské náměstí 39, Prague 1.
Tel: 26 43 62 or 36 78 22 (airport).

LUFTHANSA
Pařížská 28, Prague 1.
Tel: 231 74 40 or 231 75 51.

SAS
Stepánská 61, Prague 1.
Tel: 22 81 41 or 36 78 17 (airport).

Swissair
Pařížská 11, Prague 1.
Tel: 232 47 07 or 36 78 09 (airport).

Photography
You can buy photographic materials in specialist shops, souvenir shops and department stores. As well as local products, there's a wide selection of internationally known brands. Minilab Studios offer a quick developing service; the quality of their work is just as good (or as bad) as it is at home. Video items and film are hard to find. You should stock up before entering Czechoslovakia.

Further Reading
Chatwin, Bruce, *Utz.* Picador.
Chwaszcza, Joachim (ed), *Insight Cityguide Prague.* Apa Publications.
Garton-Ash, Timothy, *We the People: The Revolution of 1989.* Granta.
Hašek, Jaroslav, *The Good Soldier Swejk.* Penguin.
Horn, Alfred. *Insight Guide: Czechoslovakia.* Apa Publications.
Kafka, Franz, *Amerika/The Trial/The Castle.* Penguin.
Kafka, Franz, *Description of a Struggle and other stories.* Penguin.
Kafka, Franz, *Diaries.* Penguin.
Kundera, Milan, *The Unbearable Lightness of Being.* Penguin.
Neruda, Jan, *Tales of the Little Quarter.* Greenwood Press.
Seifert, Jaroslav, *Selected Poetry.* André Deutsch.
Vaculík, Ludvík, *A Cup of Coffee with my Interrogator.* Readers International.

Vaculík, Ludvík, *Prague Chronicles*.
Readers International.

Pronunciation

Vowels
á, é, í, ó, ů, ý

Long vowels
ou Like English 'show'
ě   yea

Consonants
č tch
ř r with a gentle voiced 'dj' sound
š sh
ž voiced 'sh', something like
   'Zsa Zsa Gabor'

Some common words
ano yes
ne   no

děkuji	thank you
prosím	please
dobré ráno	good morning
dobrý den	good day
dobrý večer	good evening
na shledanou	goodbye
promiňte	excuse me
co to stojí	how much, how many?
dejte mi	give me
chtěl bych	I'd like
jak dlouho	how far
jak daleko	how long
dobrý	good
spatný	bad
levný	cheap
drahý	expensive
horký	hot
studený	cold
volný	free
obsazený	taken, occupied
otevreno	open
zavreno	closed
nerozumín	I don't understa
vinárna	wine-cellar
pivnice	beer pub

ART & PHOTO CREDITS

Photography	**Hansjörg Künzel** *and* **Alfred Horn**
9, 17, 69B	**V Barl**
10, 14, 38, 39, 48, 70, 73, 77	**Bildagentur Jürgens**
18, 56, 57	**Bodo Bondzio**
21, 37, 42B, 45, 55B, 62, 67, 87, 90	**D Siegler**
26T, 27, 30	**K Vlček**
31, 49B, 50B, 60, 76	**K U Müller**
52	**Jan Sagl**
43, 47, 50T, 80	**R M Anzenberger/Jan Sagl**
51	**R M Anzenberger/Mirek Frank**
61	**R M Anzenberger/Heimo Aga**
54	**Jaroslav Kubec**
Publisher	**Hans Höfer**
Design Concept	**V Barl**
Cover Design	**Klaus Geisler**
Managing Editor	**Andrew Eames**
Production Editor	**Gareth Walters**
Cartography	**Berndtson & Berndtson**

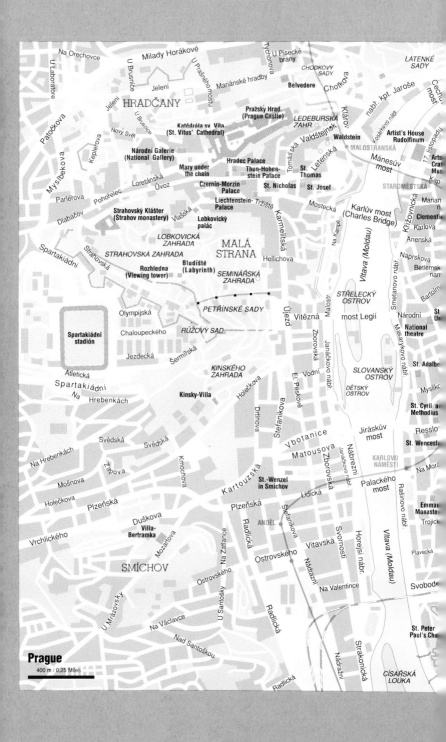

Prague

400 m / 0,25 Miles

Na Orechovce
U Laboratoře
Patočkova
Myslbekova
Keplerova
Parléřova
Pohořelec
Diabačov
Spartakiádní

Milady Horákové
U Brusnice
Jeleni
Jeleni
Nový Svět
Loretánská
Úvoz
Strahovský Klášter
(Strahov monastery)
Strahovská
LOBKOVICKÁ
ZAHRADA
STRAHOVSKÁ ZAHRADA
Rozhledna
(Viewing tower)
Vlašská
Olympijská
Chaloupeckého
Jezdecká
Šeřmířská
Atletická
Spartakiádní
Na
Hrebenkách
Svědská
Svědská
Na Hrebenkách
Mošnova
Holečkova
Plzeňská
Vrchlického

U Brusnice
U Prašného mostu
U Pražského mostu
Mariánské hradby
HRADČANY
Katédrala sv. Víta
(St. Vitus' Cathedral)
Národní Galerie
(National Gallery)
Mary under
the chain
Czernín-Morzin
Palace
Liechtenstein-
Palace
Lobkovický
palác
Bludiště
(Labyrinth)
RŮŽOVÝ SAD
KINSKÉHO
ZAHRADA
Kinsky-Villa
Štefánikova
Drtinova
Kmochova
Na Zemova
Mozartova
Duškova
Villa-
Bertramka
SMÍCHOV
U Mrázovský
Na Václavce
Nad Santoškou

Trychonova
U Pisecké
brány
CHODKOVY
SADY
Belvedere
Pražský Hrad
(Prague Castle)
LEDEBURSKÁ
ZAHR.
Tomášská
Hradec Palace
Thun-Hohen-
stein Palace
Tržiště
Karmelitská
MALÁ
STRANA
Hellichova
SEMINÁŘSKÁ
ZAHRADA
PETŘÍNSKÉ SADY
Újezd
Vítězná
Zborovská
Janáčkovo náb.
Vodní
El. Peškové
Zborovská
V'botanice
Matousova
Zborovská
Kartouzská
St.-Wenzel
in Smichov
Lidická
Plzeňská
Štefánikova
ANDĚL
Radlická
Ostrovského
Ostrovského
U Santošky
U Zátlance
Radlická
Radlická

Chotkova
Klárov
Valdštejnská
Waldstein
St.
Letenská
St. Thomas
St. Nicholas
Mostecká
St. Josef
Na Kampě
Vltava (Moldau)
Na Kampě
STŘELECKÝ
OSTROV
most Legií
SLOVANSKÝ
OSTROV
DĚTSKÝ
OSTROV
Jiráskův
most
Náb'ezní
Palackého
most
Svornosti
Vitavská
Nádraží
Na Valentince
Nádraží
Strakonická

LATENKÉ
SADY
Cechu
most
nábř. kpt. Jaroše
Kosařkovo náb.
Artist's House
Rudolfinum
MALOSTRANSKÁ
Mánesův
most
STARÓMĚSTSKÁ
Karlův most
(Charles Bridge)
Mostecká
Smetanovo náb.
Masarykovo náb.
Národní
National
theatre
St. Adalbe
Myslikc
St. Cyril a
Methodius
Resslo
St. Wencesl.
KARLOVO
NÁMĚSTÍ
Na Morá
Rašínovo nábř.
Emma
Monaste
Trojick
Vltava (Moldau)
Plavecká
Svobod
St. Peter
Paul's Chu
CÍSAŘSKÁ
LOUKA

17. listopadu
Arts
Cra
Mus
Kap
Marian
n
Clementi
Karlova
Anenská
Naprskova
Betlemsk
nam
Bartolm
St
U
Krížovnicka

Spartakiádní
stadión

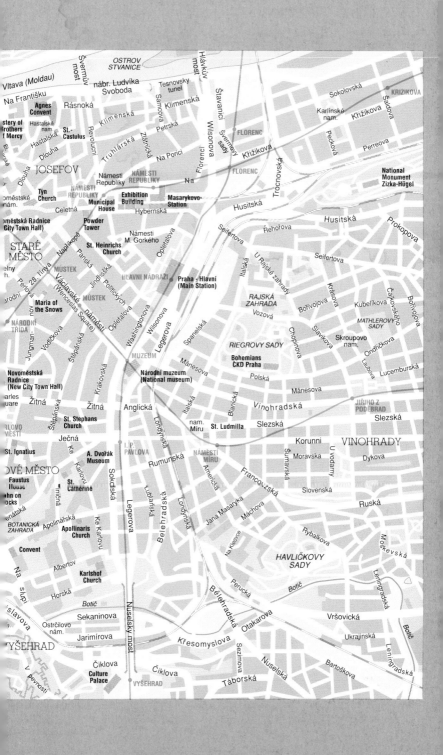

Vltava (Moldau)

Na Františku

Agnes Convent

stery of Brothers f Mercy

Rásnoká

Hastalská nam.

St.-Castulus

JOSEFOV

Týn Church

oměstské nám.

STARÉ MĚSTO

ěstská Radnice City Town Hall)

NÁMĚSTÍ REPUBLIKY

Powder Tower

St. Heinrichs Church

MÚSTEK

Václavské náměstí (Wenceslas Square)

MÚSTEK

Maria of the Snows

NÁRODNÍ TRIDA

Novoměstská Radnice (New City Town Hall)

Žitná

St. Stephans Church

Ječná

St. Ignatius

VÉ MĚSTO

Faustus House

St. Cathérine

BOTANICKÁ ZAHRADA

Convent

Karlshof Church

Botič

Sekaninova

Jarimírova

VYŠEHRAD

Čiklova

Culture Palace

OSTROV STVANICE

nábr. Ludvíka Svoboda

Tesnovsky tunel

Klimenská

Štavanicí

Hlávkův most

Klimenská

Petrská

Na Porici

Florenc

FLORENC

Křižíkova

Na

Masarykovo-Station

Hybernská

Husitská

Náměstí M. Gorkého

Opletalova

HLAVNÍ NÁDRAZÍ

Praha - Hlavní (Main Station)

Washingtonova

Wilsonova

Legerova

MUZEUM

Mánesova

Národní muzeum (National museum)

Anglická

nam. Miru

St. Ludmilla

I. P. PAVLOVA

Rumunská

NÁMĚSTÍ MIRU

Americká

Lublaňská

Sokolská

Legerova

Belehradská

Nuselský most

Křesomyslova

Sokolovská

Karlínské nam.

Křižíkova

Šaldova

Pečková

Perreova

National Monument Zizka-Hügel

Husitská

Prokopova

Řehořova

Seifertova

Italská

U Rajské zahrady

Seifertova

RAJSKÁ ZAHRADA

Vozová

Bořivojova

Krásova

Kubelíkova

Čajkovského

MATHLEROVY SADY

Bořivojova

RIEGROVY SADY

Bohemians ČKD Praha

Polská

Mánesova

Slavíkova

Ondříčkova

Skroupovo nam.

Laibova

Lucemburská

Vinohradská

JIRIHO Z PODEBRAD

Slezská

Korunni

U vodárny

VINOHRADY

Moravska

Dykova

Francouzská

Slovenská

Ruská

Jana Masaryka

Máchova

Rybalkova

Moskevská

Na Kleovce

HAVLÍČKOVY SADY

Perucká

Botič

Leningradská

Vršovická

Botič

Ukrajinská

Leningradská

Nuselská

Táborská

Bartoškova

Čiklova

VYŠEHRAD